Vancouver and Its Writers

Alan Twigg

Harbour Publishing

DEDICATION

to Betty and Art
two Vancouverites

VANCOUVER AND ITS WRITERS

Published by:
HARBOUR PUBLISHING CO. LTD.
P.O. Box 219, Madeira Park, BC Canada V0N 2H0

Design by Gaye Hammond.
Cover photo courtesy UBC Library, Special Collections.
Typeset by Penny Goldsmith and Mary White.
Printed in Canada by Friesen Printers, Altona, Manitoba.

This book was published in celebration of Vancouver's Centennial with the financial assistance of the Vancouver Centennial Commission.

CANADIAN CATALOGUING IN PUBLICATION DATA

Twigg, Alan, 1952–
    Vancouver and its writers

    Includes index.
    ISBN 0-920080-77-4

    1. Authors, Canadian (English)—British Columbia—
Vancouver—Biography.* 2. Literary landmarks—British
Columbia—Vancouver. 3. Canadian literature (English)—
British Columbia—Vancouver—History and criticism.
*I. Title.
PS8133.V3T85 1986   C810'.9'971133   C86-091271-X
PR9184.3.T85 1986

TABLE OF CONTENTS

This book has been organized in the form of a loose circle tour of the city of Vancouver and surrounding areas. It begins with the Pauline Johnson Monument in Stanley Park and moves out through the West End, crossing the Burrard Bridge and continuing west through Kitsilano and Point Grey. The tour travels back through South Vancouver to East Vancouver, Burnaby and New Westminster before returning to the Downtown area. Then to Stanley Park again to cross the Lions Gate Bridge to the North Shore, ending up at the Malcolm Lowry Walk in Dollarton.

FOREWORD

The most obvious conclusion to be drawn from this first volume of *Vancouver and Its Writers* (devoted to fiction makers) is that the Brits, throughout most of Vancouver's first century, have been dominant.

It's not called British Columbia by accident.

The second most obvious conclusion is that the Brits are no longer dominant.

"I suppose I felt British until about 1950," said John Cornish, one of Vancouver's few native-born novelists. Now the influx of sophisticated Americans such as Jane Rule, Audrey Thomas, Crawford Kilian and Keith Maillard and the ascendancy of BC-born writers such as George Bowering, Jack Hodgins, Anne Cameron, Robert Harlow, Brian Fawcett and Joy Kogawa have radically altered the literary climate of British Columbia

Meanwhile we are stuck with an arguably inappropriate name for our province and have to endure unduly habitual British values.

At my high school in West Vancouver, our basketball team was called the Highlanders. Everyone in our school wore tartan shorts. Only in my final year at school did it begin to dawn upon me to wonder how my friends of Japanese, Chinese, Jewish, German or East Indian ancestry must have felt running around the track in the red, Scottish plaid uniforms that distinguished our school from others.

Now after ten years as a literary critic, following a rewarding process that has led me to increasingly take local and contemporary literature seriously, I have likewise begun to question the effects that an excellent but British-based education system have had on the literary values of the place where I was born and have always lived.

Compiling *Vancouver and Its Writers* has alerted me to the extent that British Columbia's lingering colonial mentality has affected the public's receptivity to its own literature, to new literature that is essentially by and about itself. When the word *local* is ascribed to a Vancouver or Victoria or a Prince George author, that word *local* invariably has a pejorative ring.

The best books, according to colonial wisdom, are written by Europeans (preferably dead Europeans). On the walls of my Grade Twelve English class were pictures of all the world's great authors—Shakespeare, Thomas Hardy, George Eliot, Charles Dickens, Thackeray, D.H. Lawrence. The only literary elective was called English Lit.

The next best books are those praised in the *New York Times*.

The next best books are from Eastern Canada.

Local books are fourth-class. The ultimate literary power base is London, England. Then New York. Then Toronto. Vancouver looks good on a postcard but it's a helluva place, until only recently, to try and develop a fiction career.

Vancouver, as the second largest English-speaking city in the country, has failed in the extreme to recognize, support and celebrate its own writers. The City of

Vancouver's progressive Social Planning Department noted in its December 1985 Discussion Paper on a Cultural Action Plan that, "More than 2,500 professional writers work in Greater Vancouver, including some of Canada's best poets, playwrights and novelists. But the literary community has a low profile, despite the remarkable recent growth of BC's book publishing industry and the creation this year of the BC Book Prizes."

Certainly the next one hundred years of Vancouver history will provide a better supportive climate for indigenous fiction. But in examining Vancouver's first century, I have come to appreciate the bitter truth beneath George Bowering's contention that, as a rule, the more closely connected to Britain a Vancouver-related author has been, the more that writer's reputation has flourished.

Backwoods idealists such as Bertrand Sinclair and Hubert Evans, who combined long and industrious careers in BC with occupations such as fishing, remain largely unknown. Whereas BC's most officially venerated writer remains Roderick Haig-Brown, a magistrate and sport fisherman who wished to be known as a professional writer. In fact, Haig-Brown's literary earnings were meagre. He relied for decades on monthly cheques from his mother back in England.

The case of Haig-Brown is important if one wants to understand the literary climate that *Vancouver and Its Writers* is cumulatively representing.

Haig-Brown's style as a reflective essayist and his cultivated image as a bona fide outdoorsman won him influential friends amongst the powerful elite of BC society. Haig-Brown filled a niche nicely. He appeared to be the ideal embodiment for British Columbia of a genuine writer: the humane English squire. Gradually his renown as the great BC writer solidified into a cultural given.

When I was wearing those plaid shorts in high school, Roderick Haig-Brown, godson of Lord Baden-Powell, founder of the Boy Scout movement, was the only British Columbia writer whose name I knew. To this day he remains the only BC writer whose residence has been purchased and preserved by the BC government. And the province's top book prize, for the year's best title contributing to the appreciation and understanding of BC, is named in his honour.

In the field of fiction, another writer with strong British connections, Malcolm Lowry, is now regarded so highly that the general public, the man on the street beneath the Birk's Clock, remains amost entirely ignorant of other BC novelists.

Academics at the University of British Columbia have continued to study Lowry ad nauseam because the British-born drunken genius already has an international reputation. One cannot further one's academic career by doing some legitimate research into a legitimately British Columbian author such as A.M. Stephen, about whom a biography is long overdue.

As well, it's worthwhile to note the premier literary critic in our midst is the indefatigable and wholly admirable George Woodcock, a man whose contributions to Canadian literature are undeniable and great, but a man who nonetheless was soaked in British and European literary traditions before his arrival in Vancouver.

The book editor of the *Province*, Geoffrey Molyneux, a literate man to whom I am greatly indebted for allowing me to publish weekly excerpts of *Vancouver and Its Writers* in his book pages, hails from England. The head of the UBC Creative Writing Department, George McWhirter, was born in Ireland. And the novelist after whom the province's top fiction prize is named, Ethel Wilson, was born of British parents in South Africa.

Given this cultural climate, where nearly everyone from British Columbia is a pioneer from somewhere else, and where British pioneers have long enjoyed administrative supremacy, how can a uniquely West Coast literature thrive?

This study reveals that one route writers of fiction have taken is to investigate and sometimes emulate native BC Indians. That trend began with the author of the first

Vancouver novel, Morley Roberts, and continues to this day.

Another route BC fiction writers have taken to express their originality is to embrace the idealistic possibilities inherent in left-wing politics. *Vancouver and Its Writers* shows that much of the best literature from Canada's western-most (most Eldorado-seeking) province has come from writers, particularly disenchanted journalists, who harbour or encourage socialist political sympathies.

Literature and art attached to native Indian culture is mostly harmless. It won't upset the pattern of colonial exploitation that began with the Hudson's Bay Company, was furthered by the CPR and continues to this day with the wholesale economic development of BC's natural resources by multi-national corporations. In fact, all that Indian mysticism is respectable. The lionization of Pauline Johnson, a phoney Indian princess who once sipped tea with Queen Victoria, speaks volumes about the types of writers British Columbia selectively chooses to celebrate.

On the other hand, overtly political literature (Birney's *Down the Long Table*, A.M. Stephen's *The Gleaming Archway*, Evans' *The Western Wall*, Irene Baird's *Waste Heritage*) tends to become buried and ignored. Even Bruce Hutchison's mildly left-leaning but excellent single novel, *The Hollow Men*, is largely unheard of today. It cannot be emphasized enough, when examining the literary climate of British Columbia, that we now live in the only province in Canada in which our provincial government has decreed all new books with sociological, economic or political content that directly relates to BC are now ineligible for the publishing subsidies provided for most other kinds of books.

Another factor that cannot be stressed enough when considering the strengths and weaknesses of Vancouver fiction is that even in 1985 the majority of fiction published by British Columbians is published by firms outside the province. As long as the judgments of artistic merit or commercial viability are made in Toronto, New York or London, as has been the case almost exclusively during the first century of Vancouver's existence, Vancouver fiction writers are at a tremendous disadvantage.

Writers are strongly tempted to ignore or disguise their "local" points of view. In a short-lived column in the *Province* in the early 1980s designed to give good advice to prospective writers, Vancouver novelist Basil Jackson advised readers *not* to use local place names. Although this subservient and, I believe, ill-advised approach would be scorned by the majority of serious fiction writers of Vancouver today, the sad truth is it was offered as well-meaning and practical advice. The largest publishing house west of Ontario, Douglas & McIntyre of Vancouver, still does not publish serious fiction.

The argument made by Blanche Howard in *Vancouver and Its Writers* that she and Carol Shields cannot find a publisher for their co-written novel, in which BC politics and BC economics are discussed in depth, is not necessarily the peevish complaint of a rejected writer. During the course of researching this book, I discovered an unpublished book by A.M. Stephen called *Dark Days Ending*, an excellent novel about communism in Vancouver, written by Stephen at the height of his maturity. The manuscript had been literally collecting dust under a bed for over forty years.

Vancouver and Its Writers has also led me to understand the extent to which frontier British Columbian society fostered anti-Oriental racist sympathies. Literature played a leading role in fomenting racial tensions so that by the time 21,000 people of Japanese ancestry—17,000 of whom were Canadian citizens—were dispossessed of their properties and incarcerated in the BC Interior, the ruling elite of BC society could genuinely believe their racist fears and hatreds were historically sound, historically justified.

The courageous decency and sagacity of Hubert Evans in publishing his novella *No More Islands*, chronicling the removal of the Japanese-Canadians, during

World War II, stands for me as the most under-rated highlight in the history of BC literature. That story began to appear in installments within months of the deportations. It's long out of print.

I would be a very happy man indeed if this book helped to encourage a series of reprints of the twenty most culturally significant and accomplished out-of-print works of fiction from BC's literary history.

Now for some descriptive words of introduction:

This is, first of all, a work of synthesis. I've tried to put together the lives of over 100 writers and their over 300 fictional works relating to Vancouver into one book.

Second, it's a work of evaluation. I analyze books and draw cumulative conclusions about Vancouver literature and Vancouver society.

Third, it's a work of popularization, of propaganda. I hope to give reading pleasure to people beneath hairdryers, on toilets, in schools, together in bed, on bus tours, and alone in libraries.

Fourth, it's a work of research, a Non-Oxford Companion that scratches the largely unscratched surface of BC literature using Vancouver as a focal point.

Fifth, it's a forum for opinions of writers about Vancouver's character and its effects on their lives.

This book is designed to help British Columbians, first and foremost, who are largely ignorant of their own literature, to approach well over 100 Vancouver-related fiction authors from the familiar ground of geographic surroundings.

My definition of Vancouver extends to anywhere within one hour's drive of the plaque near Victory Square that marks the spot where surveyor L.R. Hamilton drove the first stake to begin the layout of the city in 1886.

One hundred literary sites are presented in geographical order for the sake of symbolic formality. In a young city where most of the architectural history has already been destroyed, interesting authors far out-number interesting landmarks.

But it's the thought that counts. I hope that if readers continually pass Morris' Second Hand store on Main Street, they will be drawn to investigate the remarkable work of D.M. Fraser. If you stroll past the palatial Kensington Place apartments (before they're demolished), you might want to read a book by Ethel Wilson.

I've included some personalities who are not primarily known as fiction authors, but who have had major effects on the Vancouver literary scene.

Vancouver and Its Writers also includes author photos, book jacket photos, a map and as much bibliographical detail as I could discreetly slip in. In the few cases where books were published by Vancouver firms, these publishing companies have been noted.

By far the greatest source of information about early Vancouver writing is the Special Collections section of the UBC Library. In March of 1986, the Vancouver Historical Society, with the aid of Special Collections at UBC, published a vast centennial bibliography of Vancouver-related materials, collected primarily by Linda Hale. That bibliography is available at most BC libraries and contains references to some of the more obscure titles I've also managed to come across.

I welcome mail, in care of Harbour Publishing. Information about early BC authors is particularly welcome. I hope future volumes, either by myself or others, can be published to spotlight Vancouver-related non-fiction authors, poets, dramatists, authors of children's books and significant literary supporters and critics.

Meanwhile I'm looking forward to an improved literary climate for fiction in my hometown in its second century. And I hope this book will appeal to the serious scholar and the curious tourist alike.

Thanks to Howard White, for having faith in me, and to Margaret Waddington and Don Stewart for so willingly providing tips. And most of all, thanks to my parents, to whom this book is dedicated, for raising two professional writers, and for separately continuing to provide unswerving and constant support.

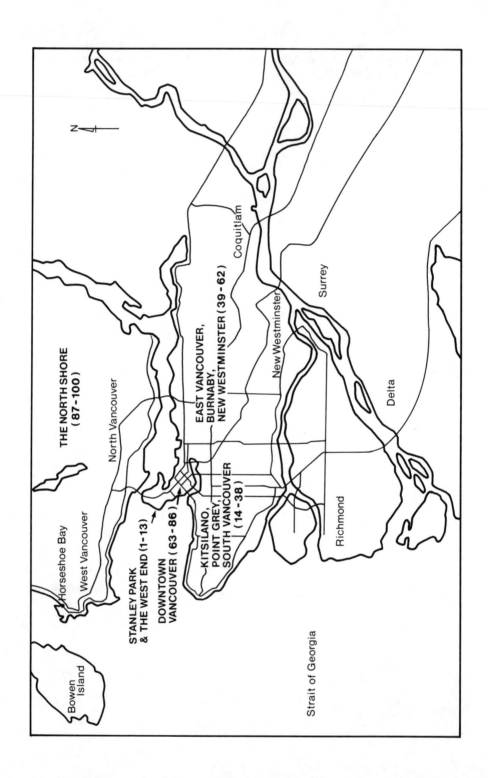

THE NORTH SHORE
(87 - 100)

Horseshoe Bay

West Vancouver

North Vancouver

STANLEY PARK
& THE WEST END (1-13)

DOWNTOWN
VANCOUVER (63 - 86)

KITSILANO,
POINT GREY,
SOUTH VANCOUVER
(14 - 38)

EAST VANCOUVER,
BURNABY,
NEW WESTMINSTER (39 - 62)

Coquitlam

New Westminster

Surrey

Delta

Richmond

Bowen
Island

Strait of Georgia

N

ONE

Pauline Johnson Monument

FERGUSON POINT, STANLEY PARK

The city of Vancouver, in its first one hundred years, has officially designated one literary landmark to honour a local author. Ironically, this memorial, erected in 1922, recalls a writer who resided in Vancouver only four years, who wrote mostly doggerel verse, and who specifically requested in her will that no such memorial be built.

Emily Pauline Johnson was born in Brantford, Ontario on March 10, 1861. She was Mohawk halfbreed born to well-to-do pro-British parents. At age thirty she adopted her career as a poet-entertainer. She dubbed herself "Tekahionwake" and adopted Indian garb for her poetry recitals.

Johnson toured extensively, mixed with London's upper classes and was received by Queen Victoria. As Canada's pre-eminent literary ambassador, Pauline Johnson did much to cultivate a romanticized notion of her homeland and native Indian culture.

Her first poetry collection, *The White Wampum* (1895), was published by the Bodley Head in London, followed by *Canadian Born* (1903) and *Flint and Feathers* (1912). In 1911 she published *Legends of Vancouver*, her transformed versions of stories told to her by her friend, Chief Joe Capilano of the Squamish Indian band. She had wanted the book titled *Legends of the Capilanos* but was convinced to change the title for marketing reasons. Two collections of prose fiction, *The Shagganappi* and *The Moccasin Maker*, appeared posthumously in 1913. Her most anthologized poem is "The Song My Paddle Sings."

When visiting the city, Pauline Johnson stayed at the Hotel Vancouver. She announced her intention to live permanently in Vancouver in 1909 before an appreciative audience at the Pender Auditorium. Eschewing her career as a pop star of her times, she took an apartment at 1117 Howe Street and concentrated on her writing. She published her Indian legends in the *Province* and became a member of the newly formed Canadian Women's Press Club.

Suffering from painful breast cancer, she expressed her desire to be buried in Stanley Park. The area was administered by the Canadian admiralty and leased to the city at the time. Wary of setting precedents, the admiralty agreed to Johnson's request with the proviso that she be cremated.

Nine days prior to her death on March 7, 1913, she

Vancouver turns out to mourn the passing of its favorite poet Pauline Johnson, 1913.

requested that no memorial be raised in her memory, adding "I particularly desire that neither my sister or brother wear black nor what is termed mourning for me, as I have always disliked such displays of personal feelings. I desire that no mourning notepaper or stationery be used by them." The Women's Canadian Club began its campaign to erect a monument in 1914. Insufficient funds delayed the project until 1922.

Initial response to the memorial was mixed. Johnson's right profile is depicted looking away from her beloved Siwash Rock and the face and braided hairstyle were not representative. Neglected during World War II, the monument was stripped of its bronze by thieves in 1945. It was desecrated with red paint in 1953. *Vancouver Sun* book columnist Don Stainsby reported the dilapidated condition of the monument in 1961. The Vancouver Parks Board refurbished the memorial in 1981.

A BIOGRAPHY OF PAULINE JOHNSON
BETTY KELLER

Pauline Johnson's sister commented in 1924, "I do not like the way Vancouver seems to claim Pauline. Pauline lived all her life in the East with the exception of about four years which were passed in Vancouver where she died." Betty Keller's comprehensive biography, *Pauline* (1981), provides the best study of Tekahionwake. Novelist Ethel Wilson recorded her impressions of Johnson in "The Princess," an article printed in *Canadian Literature* in 1981.

"Tekahionwake," the Indian name of Johnson's great-grandfather, means Double Wampum. When the editor of the *Vancouver World* newspaper received a $225 share from the sales of *Legends of Vancouver* in 1915 from the poet's sister, he later used the money to launch a subscription fund to buy a gun for the 29th Battalion during World War I. After enormous public response, the necessary $1,000 was raised and the gun was delivered to the troops. On the gun barrel was inscribed the word, "Tekahionwake."

TWO

Coal Harbour

STANLEY PARK

Here, at the Royal Vancouver Yacht Club, the yacht *Spindrift* was moored at the outset of Stewart Edward White's two coastal novels, *Skookum Chuck* (1925) and *Secret Harbour* (1926).

Stewart Edward White was born in Grand Rapids, Michigan on March 12, 1883. He was educated at University of Michigan and Columbia University. He married in 1904 and resided mostly in California. As a journalist he made several forays up the West Coast before turning to producing books for a living. The urbane characters in his two comic adventure novels that begin in Vancouver suggest he was an unusually philosophical and sophisticated personality.

In *Skookum Chuck* the reader meets Roger Marshall, a handsome and aloof middle-aged American who is inexplicably stricken with a profound indifference to life. In Vancouver he visits a "healer of souls" named X. Anaxagoras who strikes an odd bargain with him. The healer will charge no fee if he can cure Marshall's apathy towards life, but will charge ten thousand dollars if he fails at the task. They take a cabin cruiser at midnight from Coal Harbour and, accompanied by the healer's acerbic sister Betsy, encounter bootlegging, intrigue, pirateering, a potlatch ceremony in the Queen Charlottes and other unforseen adventures. Marshall regains his appetite for life.

The sequel to *Skookum Chuck* is *Secret Harbour*. Marshall and Betsy are married and living on the *Spindrift*. Anaxagoras returns as the cryptic-altruistic-con-artist-cum-psychic-healer-of-souls-and-psychologist-oracle. He persuades Marshall he's too perfect, too safe, too dull, too much of a prisoner of The Proper Thing aboard his luxury yacht. Ludicrous adventures ensue. Tossing overboard all nautical discipline and propriety, the cast of the *Spindrift* kidnap two greedy characters named Fleshpots and Eat's-em-alive. Anaxagoras successfully claim-jumps a gold mine. "Adventure always come to one who goes forth with the spirit of adventure within him," writes White. "An adventure is always a release. It makes fluid what has solidified into rigidity. It permits infiltration." He goes on to say, "We sail our surface seas of life, but only rarely are we privileged to glimpse the deeps where continents are forming for future nobler races. And then we rarely look."

Stewart Edward White wrote over forty-five other books. The date of his death is unknown.

THREE

Nine O'Clock Gun

STANLEY PARK

A novel by Roland Wild, *The Nine O'Clock Gun* (1952), named after this gun placement, is a semi-historical compilation of Vancouver stories and personalities. In tracing the fortunes of a fictional Scottish immigrant, the author weaves a tale from the boisterous boom-town days of Gassy Jack Deighton to the repressive civic administration of Mayor Gerry McGeer. The Nine O'Clock Gun was fired to mark the beginning and closing of fishing hours in Burrard Inlet. With so many unemployed men trying to make a living by fishing, the canneries needed to restrict fishing to prevent over-supply. The citizens of Vancouver began to depend on the gun to set their watches.

Roland Wild was born on August 7, 1903 in Lancashire, England. As a journalist he worked for three years in the Punjab for the newspaper that had previously employed Rudyard Kipling. "American tourists were always coming into the office looking to buy mementos. I'd tell them if they came back in three or four hours I might be able to dig up Kipling's chair. We had an excellent carpenter in the back!" He later published a biography of an Indian Prince who was also a renowned cricketer, *Ranji* (1935) and a biography of famous criminal lawyer Sir Henry Curtis-Bennett, *Curtis* (1936). His first novel, *The Trial of Mary Court* (1939) was about a murder trial in London's Old Bailey. During the war Wild worked in psychological warfare, printing newspapers in German for the German population. In this capacity he met many Canadians, many of whom were homesick, particularly the British Columbians. He decided to emigrate in 1947.

In his first week in Vancouver, Wild took a job with the *Vancouver Herald*. For many years he was solely responsible for the editorial page. "I'd write something about Russia, look up at the window and write something else, toss in a syndicated piece by Dorothy Thompson and pick some letters to the editor. Then I went and played a game of golf. I'd come back in the evenings for twenty minutes to read the proofs. My editor never changed a word. I never enjoyed myself so much." When the *Herald* folded, Wild became one of four editorial writers for the *Province*. His biography of early BC premier William Alexander Smith, *Amor de Cosmos* (1958), was published to mark the 100th anniversary of the newspaper Amor de Cosmos founded, *The Victoria Colonist*. He also wrote a book about Captain Smellie, who each year sailed with supplies into the Arctic from Montreal, *Arctic Command* (1964), and a book on golf, *The Loneliest Game* (1969). A long and ambitious novel, inspired by his visit to the Angkor Wat ruins in Cambodia in 1964, has not been published.

Retired and living in West Vancouver, Wild is a stringer for one of the world's largest newspapers, the *London Daily Telegraph*. "Of course that doesn't mean very much," he notes. "If Vancouver slid into the sea tomorrow they might give me two paragraphs."

FOUR
Brockton Point

STANLEY PARK

In Robert Allison Hood's novel, *The Chivalry of Keith Leicester* (1919), the hero escorts the heroine to Brockton Point on horseback where he explains at some length why Pauline Johnson is the Walter Scott of Vancouver.

Robert Allison Hood was born on March 20, 1880 at Cupar, Fife in Scotland. He came to California with his mother and brother in 1893. After graduating from the University of California in 1906, he came to Vancouver to work in real estate and insurance. A confirmed British chauvinist, Robert Hood wrote romantic potboilers of his era. In his first novel, Keith Leicester is a BC rancher who believes he is a misogynist. Marjorie, an English girl, arrives to work for a nearby rancher and soon elicits chivalry from the hard-as-nails rancher from "Portlake, BC" who also happens to harbour a deep admiration for the poetry of Pauline Johnson. Marjorie is mistaken for a jewel thief while staying at the Hotel Vancouver. Leicester comes to her defence and takes responsibility for and custody of Marjorie until the matter is cleared up.

They paddle a canoe to Ferguson Point and recognize their mutual loneliness, ride horses around Brockton Point, and rest at Ferguson Point. There Leicester tactfully professes his love and describes the harbour as "the Sunset Doorway of the Dominion." All ends happily when Marjorie turns out to be independently wealthy. The couple is prepared to heroically forego a comfortable life in England in favour of a much less lucrative but richer life in the West.

Hood's other BC novel is *The Quest of Alistair* (1921). His third novel, *The Case of Kinnear* (1942), is set in Scotland. He also published two collections of terrible verse.

FIVE
Lumberman's Arch

STANLEY PARK

The writer whom Margaret Laurence has dubbed "the elder of our tribe" proposed to his wife in 1920 under

5

Hubert Evans

the former site of Lumberman's Arch (since destroyed and replaced).

Hubert Evans was born on May 9, 1892 in Vankleek Hill, Ontario. The son of a stern Methodist schoolteacher, Evans wrote and fantasized in his boyhood about paddling away from home in his canoe to live with the Indians. His three younger brothers were to pursue esteemed professional careers but he chose to drop out of school to take his first job as a reporter for the *Galt Reporter* in 1910. Further newspaper jobs in Toronto, New Westminster and Nelson honed his appreciation for concise, unprejudiced prose. He served in the trenches of World War I as a messenger for three years, was wounded at Ypres, and discharged in 1919. On the train west to visit his parents in New Westminster, he met a Fisheries chief who offered him a lucrative public relations job. Instead, Evans asked for a job as a northern BC fish hatchery attendant.

He corresponded with a Galt schoolgirl friend, Ann Winter, who shared his idealistic tendencies. "I knew my wife ever since we were thirteen and we both always had the same idea. To travel light. To own only what you can carry on your back." In 1920 the couple were married by a minister from the Mt. Pleasant Methodist Church but both later chose to become Quakers. Evans built a floathouse at his Cultus Lake salmon hatchery with the help of local Indians and sold a 500 word satirical piece to Dorothy Parker at the *New Yorker* to begin his long freelance career. "It was a thing about a high-pressured business executive who had retired to the country. His hobby was keeping bees. He used the same technique on the bees as he had used to manage his sales staff. It ended with the bees stinging him to death—which must have suited Dorothy Parker just fine."

The Evanses lived briefly at Dundarave in West Vancouver, and in North Vancouver. His first book, *Forest Friends* 1926, was a collection of carefully observed nature anecdotes, published in Phladelphia. "I couldn't write about violence so I wrote outdoor stories." While living on Carisbrooke Road in North Van, the couple bought a lot with 100 feet of ocean frontage at Roberts Creek, BC. There, in 1927, Evans built the house where he would live and work as a professional writer for nearly sixty years.

His first adult novel, *The New Front Line* (1927), is the story of a war weary veteran who escapes the "old front line" of battle to homestead in British Columbia. Evans' three novels for juveniles about his airedale retriever (*Airedale of the Frontier*, 1928; *Derry's Partner*, 1929; *Derry of Totem Creek*, 1930) and another nature collection, *The Silent Call* (1930) appeared prior to the "seven lean years" of the Depression. Evans took up commercial fishing in earnest, wrote left wing plays, taught unemployed men to fish, explored the coast on a twenty-eight foot "rum runner" called "The Solheim" (which accommodated his family and a small piano) and turned increasingly to short stories.

In 1932 he published possibly the best of his approximately sixty novellas and serials, *The Western Wall*, about the spiritual and political questioning of an unemployed Vancouver garage mechanic literally adrift on an open sea when he is forced to take up hand trolling off Bowen Island. During World War II Evans vigorously fought a propaganda campaign for pacifist ideals by publishing inspirational short stories and serials for juveniles in denominational magazines. "My wife said she'd rather have me digging ditches than writing pulp. She suggested I write for teenagers because you can still change a person's viewpoint up to the time they're twenty."

In 1942 Evans published *No More Islands*, the first book to seriously examine the expulsion of Japanese-Canadians from the BC coast, presenting a variety of viewpoints while empathizing with the rights of the Japanese-Canadians whom Evans and his wife knew first hand.

After living almost eight years in Indian villages, Evans published *Mist on the River* (1954), his second adult novel and the first Canadian novel to realistically depict native Indians as central characters. "I could have written about the injustices Indians faced. I've seen all that. But I had commercial-fished and trapped and built dugout canoes with these people. I could roll a cigarette and sit on my heels and talk with them. I was one of them. I wanted to show how they were really just like us. Basically I was just being a reporter."

Now revered as a Canadian classic and re-issued, *Mist on the River* led to the publication of a juvenile novel about an Indian boy coping with the encroachment of white entrepreneuring in his village, *Mountain Dog* (1956). This book was republished in 1981 as *Son of the Salmon People*. Evans' other major work for young readers is a biography of David Thompson's formative years, *North to the Unknown* (1949), which emphasizes the great mapmaker's "pathfinding" as a spiritual as well as a physical exploration.

Ann Winter Evans died after a long illness in 1960. A second "depression" created another publishing drought. Sixteen years later, buoyed by the correspondence of Margaret Laurence and the friendship of local publisher Howard White, Harbour Publishing published three books of his poetry, *Whittlings* (1976), *Endings* (1978), and *Mostly Coast People* (1982). In his 80s and stricken by serious ailments, Evans resisted near-blindness and numerous heart operations to compose his most remarkable book and his third adult

Writers Alan Twigg, Howard White, Edith Iglauer and John Faustmann at impromptu wake for Hubert Evans, Roberts Creek, June 1986.

novel, *O Time in Your Flight,* published by Harbour in 1979. The book is a scrupulously remembered account of the year the twentieth century began as viewed through the eyes of a nine year old boy in Ontario. He wrote each day, a few hundred words at a time, using a system of three tape recorders—one for notes, one for a rough draft, and one for a final draft. Typing made him dizzy but with five per cent vision, holding his nose inches from the keyboard, he independently completed the manuscript. *O Time in Your Flight* has been widely praised and was one of the final novels aired on the CBC program "Booktime."

The Simon Fraser University Convocation Party made a special trip to Evans' seaside home on February 3rd, 1984, accompanied by Ontario novelist Margaret Laurence, to bestow an honourary doctorate of law degree on Evans. The annual Hubert Evans Prize for Non-Fiction was established in 1985 to recognize the province's superior work of non-fiction. A critical study and biography, *Hubert Evans, The First Ninety-Three Years* (1985) was written by the author of this book. Evans died in the spring of 1986, a few weeks after his ninety-fourth birthday.

SIX

Whale Pool

VANCOUVER AQUARIUM, STANLEY PARK

"The whale pool had much to do with my book, *Not Wanted on the Voyage,* because it was there I had my first unhappy close-ups of whales: unhappy because I can never be reconciled to animals being held in captivity unless it is protective captivity in the case of species that are endangered in the wild. Two days after I had seen the whales, the young Beluga died and I remember laying flowers in his memory on the ledge of the window through which you can see the whales underwater," recalls Timothy Findley. He later adapted the Noah's Ark myth to express his fears for the future of the planet and animalkind in *Not Wanted on the Voyage.* "I went back to the aquarium the next day but the flowers were gone. I've always wondered where they went to. Maybe someone took them out and put them in the sea."

Timothy Findley was born October 30, 1930 in Toronto. He was a professional actor for fifteen years, at Stratford and abroad, before devoting himself to writing fulltime in 1962. His novels are *The Last of the Crazy People* (1967), *The Butterfly Plague* (1969), *The*

Wars (1977), *Famous Last Words* (1981) and *Not Wanted on the Voyage* (1984). *The Wars* received a Governor General's Award and became a film directed by Robin Phillips. Findley is an ardent conservationist and animal lover. He lives on an Ontario farm dubbed The Stone Orchard with an animal menagerie that includes over twenty cats.

Findley first visited Vancouver in 1972 with William Whitehead to research their adaptation of Pierre Berton's *The National Dream* and *The Last Spike* into an eight hour television drama. He has returned many times, once as Chairman of the Writers Union of Canada, and once to deliver a radical, anti-industrial-exploitation speech to the Vancouver Institute at UBC before an overflow audience of over 1,000 in 1985. Only the Dalai Lama and Margaret Atwood have attracted equal Vancouver crowds for Institute lectures. "As an easterner, my impression of Vancouver has always been as a city by the water, with Japanese gardens blooming in the mist. The sight of the harbours, bays and mountains is a magical reviver of the spirit." Findley says he likes to go on buying sprees at Duthie's, Murchie's and Bootlegger ("the best bandana handkerchiefs in the world") but he especially enjoys visiting Vancouver's surrounding islands. "Even though Saltspring and places like that are beyond Vancouver, they *are* Vancouver to me, if only in my mind, because I cannot be in Vancouver without wanting to be beneath the trees in Cathedral Grove or walking the beach at Pacific Sands near Tofino. One is always the promise of the other."

SEVEN

Second Beach

STANLEY PARK

Keath Fraser

In the title story of Keath Fraser's *Foreign Affairs* (1985), the best work of fiction ever produced by a native Vancouverite, a fifty year old ex-diplomat afflicted with multiple sclerosis struggles against the constraints of his live-in nurse to take wheelchair "holiday" outings along the Stanley Park seawall to Second Beach, accompanied by a coarse-tongued, anorexic, punk-woman named Nadine.

Keath Fraser is Vancouver's most promising fiction writer, born in Vancouver on December 24, 1944. The remarkable range of his stories has already drawn high praise from the country's most discriminating critics. He has travelled extensively throughout the world, lived in

9

London, England from 1970–73 and taught in Calgary for five years. He gave up a tenured position teaching university English and began writing fiction full-time in 1980, returning to live in Vancouver where his wife is a teacher.

His first collection of stories, *Taking Cover* (1982) prompted *Canadian Fiction Magazine* to devote an entire issue, number 49, to publishing two of his novellas. His work has been recognized relatively quickly by his peers and the country's leading literary magazines but Fraser remains almost unheralded in his hometown. "The *Vancouver Sun* is just pitiful, the book pages they have. It's just tragic, the lack of solicitation to local writers. We are now getting reviews by Margaret Atwood which I read one week in the *New York Times*, appearing the next week in the *Vancouver Sun*. So we are getting book reviews by Canadian writers now through the filter of cheaper, American wire services. Until that situation improves at our largest newspaper, local recognition of our writers isn't going to improve either."

Fraser's stories are primarily set in Vancouver and are assertively local to an unprecedented degree. Only Vancouver readers can possibly catch all the nuances of offhand references to personalities such as Tony Parsons, Ron Zalko or Chunky Woodward, or locales mentioned casually and without explanation. ("I pinch the odd tie off Chunky Woodward but listen. It stops there, eh?") His style is deeply serious and condensive, apparently colloquial and slapdash, yet riveting and strange, as he invites his reader into a maze of clues which cumulatively evolve into a non-linear story.

The diversity of characters and approaches to storytelling in *Foreign Affairs*, and his original prose techniques, prompted Toronto critic Ken Adachi to recommend the book for a Governor General's Award in the *Toronto Star*. The first story, "Waiting," enters the mind of a Vancouver Hindu who is a waiter in a high class French restaurant. "The Emerald City" unravels the turmoil of an adulterous TV gardening show host. "Teeth" is about a fatal camping expedition by two retired brothers in mobile homes who encounter a bizarre sect in the woods north of Pemberton. "13 Ways of Listening to a Stranger" captures the communal atmosphere of a Vancouver boarding house where the male residents unite each evening to watch the CTV evening news.

The best and longest story, "Foreign Affairs," succeeds in making attractive the complex problems of a frustrated invalid and the confused social alienation of his waifish, punk-haired companion. Passing the English Bay bathhouse during Sea Festival, "His gaze is determined to covet everything. The filmy blouses of thin-strapped, heavy-breasted girls in white jeans and black heels. Helium balloons shaped like silver salmon tied to the wrists of oriental infants. Bowling pins in the air around a juggler's head. The mincing steps of male couples in pressed jeans and white sneakers. Sloops and yawls of drinking revelers anchored offshore in the twilight. An apricot sky turning tomato, and the mountains of Vancouver Island standing up to a pink apocalypse.''

Fraser is understandably concerned that the literary culture of Vancouver has yet to cohere and his reputation at home is almost non-existent. Besides blaming the *Vancouver Sun*, he describes the cultural policies of the BC provincial government as "philistine. It's pitiful when you think that I'm getting more money, more support, from the government of Ontario than I'll ever get out of the government of BC. When you consider that we have such a strong artistic constituency on the West Coast, it's absurd.'' But he is simultaneously devoted to local turf. "I can't imagine living elsewhere and trying to write about it. For all the drawbacks, this is a privileged place to be for a writer. It's such virgin territory.''

In 1986 Fraser is tending an infant son and completing a novel. He is a close literary friend of Sinclair Ross.

Born in a homestead near Prince Albert, Saskatchewan in 1908, one of Canada's most significant novelists, **Sinclair Ross**, now lives in obscurity in the Shaughnessy district. "I would be grateful if you ignored me," he said in 1985. "You see, I have Parkinson's Disease. I don't speak well. There are things that enter my mind to say but I don't trust myself to say them. If you came to see me, I'm afraid it might be unpleasant for you.''

Ross' landmark contribution to Canadian literature is his novel, *As For Me and My House*. "For a long time I've felt that *As For Me and My House* never amounted to much. It was alright at the time. But I feel the world has changed so much...If I was starting out again I think I'd concentrate on the novella. Ideas enter my head from time to time but I no longer think of myself as a writer...If you wrote about me in your book it might make some people want to visit me. And I don't want that...I came to Vancouver about three years ago. I don't know the city well.''

Ross has also published three other novels, *The Well* (1958), *Whir of Gold* (1970) and *Sawbones Memorial* (1974). Two short story collections, *The Lamp at Noon and Other Stories* (1968) and *The Race and Other Stories* (1982) have also been published.

EIGHT

English Bay

"Vancouver is the end of my quest. Here it is—The Promised Land. After Prague, New York, Washington, Vienna, Munich and Mysore City, I finally found it. I was thirty when I settled here in 1965 and except for an occasional research trip I haven't been away. There is the breathtaking impact of the North Shore mountains and the excitement of a society being born on the shores of the world's largest ocean, among so many other reasons for being elated with my choice. For someone who spent the first thirteen years of his life in a landlocked country (I first saw the sea in Dieppe in 1948), the idea of living next door to English Bay will never stop being exotic."

k.o. kanne, Alan Twigg, Trevor Carolan, Jan Drabek

Jan Drabek was born in Prague, Czechoslovakia on May 5, 1935. His father was a lawyer-journalist active in the Czech underground during WW II. Drabek Sr., although not Jewish, was sent to Auschwitz in 1943 with "Return Unwanted" stamped on his papers. He survived to become chief prosecutor of a Czechoslovak war crimes tribunal and a commentator for "Voice of America." In 1984 Drabek accompanied his father, Jaroslav Drabek, to Auschwitz for the filming of a twenty minute memoir, *Father's Return to Auschwitz*, directed by Czech-born Ivan Horsky.

Jan Drabek came to Vancouver with a plan to drive down the West Coast in search of work as a journalist. But his wife's family was already in Vancouver, as was a Czech botanist who had headed his father's underground group. Drabek stayed and taught high school in Kitsilano and wrote a non-fiction book called *Blackboard Odyssey* (1973) about his experience.

Drabek is the author of four novels: *Whatever Happened to Wenceslas?* (1975), *Report on the Death of Rosenkavalier* (1977), *The Lister Legacy* (1980) and *The Statement* (1982). A forthcoming novel is entitled *The Cucumber Season*. All these books, with the exception of *The Lister Legacy*, contain Vancouver settings or references, although Drabek is best known for stories set against the backdrop of global politics.

Like his fellow Czech emigre novelist Josef Skvorecky, Drabek feels obliged to wake North American society from a slumber of innocence with regards to the potential threats of totalitarian or communist regimes. *The Statement*, for example, recounts how a political science professor at UBC engineers a revolution in a fictitious country called New Salisbury. "One of the most difficult points for us English-speaking people to grasp is that *we* are the aberration," says Drabek's radicalized professor, "and that the dictatorships and police states are much more the normal thing in the world."

Jan Drabek, in 1985-86, is the chairman of the Federation of BC Writers.

NINE

Hotel Sylvia

1154 GILFORD STREET

East of the Johnson monument is the Sylvia lounge, Vancouver's perennial favourite haunt for writers and visiting literati. "In this society," claims frequent patron George Payerle, "bars serve the function of churches. People go to pray, gossip and find communion. Among the surviving older bars, the Sylvia is perhaps the most quintessentially 'Vancouver.' "

One of the few authors in this book who was born in Vancouver, **George Payerle** was born on August 21, 1945. He attended the University of British Columbia for seven years and published a short experimental novel, *The Afterpeople* (1970), subtitled, "a patheticon." This minor work is a montage of unfathomable events arising from a bank robbery at the Granville and Pender branch of the Bank of Montreal. "If I can be said to write 'about' anything," Payerle wrote, seven years later, "I write about perception; or, I write perception. Good writing is like wine or blood, depending on the mood you're in." His forthcoming novel is set partially in the Sylvia lounge, which Payerle admires for being "like the hotel itself, seedily graceful, mixing the genteel and ordinary to the enhancement of both."

The distinction of being Vancouver's first native-born novelist goes to **Alfred Batson**, born in 1900. As an infant he probably lived at 1142 Hornby Street, an address listed in a turn-of-the-century directory as the residence of C.F. Batson, a sailor. Alfred Batson grew up in Boston, Massachusetts but he served in the Canadian army in World War I. He then fought as a captain with the rebel forces in Nicaragua until the US Marines re-established control and he was forced to flee overland to Mexico. Batson's only known novel is *African Intrigue* (1933), an account of Franco-German rivalry in Africa. Probably observed first hand, the conflict in the story emphasizes that native peoples invariably suffer most when two international powers battle for territory. The whereabouts and fate of Batson are unknown.

13

TEN

Muckamuck

RESTAURANT (now QUILICUM), 1724 DAVIE STREET

Helen Potrebenko, one of Vancouver's most uncompromising feminist writers, picketed here on the sidewalk for over two years.

Helen Potrebenko was born on June 21, 1940 in Woking, Alberta. After arriving in Vancouver to attend university, she documented the struggles of a female cab driver to earn a living in her novel *Taxi*, published by New Star Books in 1975. "It just never occurs to them we're people and not zoo animals to be stared at," the narrator writes, "and that we have feelings and don't like being prodded and mauled by thirty different guys in one day."

Potrebenko's second book, *No Streets of Gold* (New Star, 1977) is a social history of Ukrainians in Alberta. Her strong collection of fiction and other writings, *A Flight of Average Persons* (New Star, 1979), voiced her defiant pride in the dignity of working class lives, particularly women disadvantaged by a patriarchal society.

Potrebenko marked the second anniversary of her participation in the strike to earn a first contract for SORWUC workers at the Muckamuck restaurant on Davie Street with the publication of *Two Years on the Muckamuck Line* (Lazara Publications, 1980). The white owners of Vancouver's first restaurant to exclusively serve West Coast native Indian cuisine ultimately left Vancouver in the strike's third year. Six workers had been fired upon the union's application for certification. The owners refused to negotiate. "The Muckamuck hired scab labour and tried to keep the restaurant open," says Potrebenko. "Scabs spent their working hours swearing, spitting and beating on picketers. Sometimes they were assisted by outside goons. When the owners finally left town, the Labour Relations Board bestirred itself to order the Muckamuck to pay a token $10,000 because of its illegal activities. This could never be collected. We've never officially called the strike off." The Quilicum Restaurant, however, is operating with the support of the union.

The title poem of Potrebenko's first book of poetry, *Walking Slow*, published by Lazara Publications in 1985, affirms her determination to keep picketing.

ELEVEN

Kensington Place

BEACH AND NICOLA AVENUES

Ethel Wilson

Ethel Wilson, Vancouver's most respected novelist for several decades, lived here in Apartment 42.

Ethel Davis Wilson was born on January 20, 1888 in Port Elizabeth, South Africa, daughter of a Wesleyan Methodist minister. She went to live in Pembroke, Wales in 1890 after her mother died. Her father died when she was nine. At age ten she was taken to live with her maternal grandmother in Vancouver. From ages fourteen to eighteen she attended a school for Methodist ministers' daughters at Trinity Hall in Southport, England. She later described this period as "rigorous, almost spartan, sound, and often very amusing." Her schoolmistress remembered her years later as "the school beauty." She returned to Vancouver, received her teacher's certificate from the Vancouver Normal School in 1907, and taught in Vancouver elementary schools, dutifully but without pleasure, until 1920.

In 1921 she found lasting security and happiness when she married Dr. Wallace Wilson, a much respected non-literary man (president of the Canadian Medical Association, chairman of its ethics committee, professor of medical ethics at UBC). "I think she was basically shy," family acquaintance Muriel Whitaker has recalled, "and her confidence came from Wallace who was gentle, genial, low-keyed and absolutely dependable." The couple lived in relative luxury in their spacious Kensington Place apartment overlooking False Creek, surrounded by Oriental rugs, books, a photo of a sketch of Winston Churchill, an original Burne-Jones pencil drawing and the same housekeeper for twenty-two years.

Ethel Wilson claimed to have written her first stories in the late 1930s in the family automobile while her husband called on the sick. *The New Statesman*, to her surprise, published her work but she stopped writing during the war. She said she wrote her first and possibly best novel, *Hetty Dorval* (1947), in three weeks while her beloved husband was away "in order to remain alive, sane and functioning." In it, an innocent girl from the BC interior, Frankie Burnaby, narrates the story of a visiting city woman named Hetty Dorval.

The Innocent Traveller (1949) is an autobiographical but unrevealing story of a young girl coming to live in Vancouver from England and remaining a relatively happy spinster past her 100th birthday. Although it

15

appears Ethel Wilson turned suddenly to fiction in her mature years, portions of *The Innocent Traveller* can be traced to preparatory writing she had started twenty years prior to its publication. *The Equations of Love* (1952) consists of two novellas, "Tuesday and Wednesday," about the death of a husband on a Wednesday, and "Lily's Story," about the resolve of an unwed mother to raise her child.

Wilson's most celebrated novel, *Swamp Angel* (1954), primarily concerns the escape of Maggie Vardoe from an unpleasant second marriage in Vancouver to a new life at a remote interior BC lake. She meets a retired circus juggler, and other uniquely non-urbanized women. Maggie Vardoe learns independence but is told near the end of the novel, "We are all in it together. 'No Man is an Iland, I am involved in Mankinde,' and we have no immunity and we may as well realize it." The novel owes many of its characters and its locale to a lodge at Lac Le Jeune where Ethel Wilson vacationed with her husband, an expert fisherman, for forty years. Lac Le Jeune was also the setting for two short stories, "On Nimpish" and "Beware the Jabberwock, my son...beware the Jubjub bird." Mr. Spencer, the character at the outset of *Swamp Angel* who buys Maggie Vardoe's hand-tied flies to facilitate her escape, was derivative of a co-owner of Vancouver's Harkley & Haywood sporting goods store. The Swamp Angel of the title is a small revolver that is discarded. Ethel Wilson herself once had the pleasant experience of tossing a small gun off a bridge. Wilson's final novel, *Love and Salt Water* (1956), is a post-WW II novel most directly concerned with private wounds and the uncertainty of human relations.

Dr. Wilson died in 1966 and Ethel Wilson moved to an apartment on Point Grey Road, suffered a stroke and no longer wrote. She lived for nearly eight years in the Arbutus Nursing Home until her death on December 22, 1980. About forty people attended a funeral service at Christ Church Cathedral. "There was no eulogy," family friend and journalist Mary McAlpine has noted, "and afterwards most of us went across the street to a special room in the Hotel Vancouver and had coffee or drinks and sandwiches, and she would have liked that." She was cremated with her favourite pictures of her late husband and his letters.

Socially well-connected, Ethel Wilson has received more recognition for her work posthumously than most other novelists indigenous to Vancouver. BC's top fiction award, The Ethel Wilson Prize for Fiction, devised in 1985, commemorates her achievements. She was the first and almost only BC fiction writer besides Malcolm Lowry to have her work serve as the subject of a full-length critical study. Desmond Pacey published *Ethel Wilson* (1968) and the University of Ottawa published the proceedings of an Ethel Wilson Symposium held in 1981.

Also living in the West End, unheralded, is the English language translator of Heinrich Boll, **Leila Vennewitz**. She lives with her husband in an apartment near Lost Lagoon, preferring a decidedly non-glamourous, non-academic life. Boll, who died in 1985, was a winner of the Nobel Prize for Literature.

TWELVE

Sunset Beach

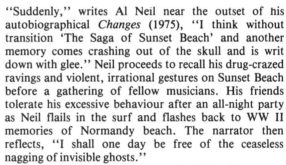

"Suddenly," writes Al Neil near the outset of his autobiographical *Changes* (1975), "I think without transition 'The Saga of Sunset Beach' and another memory comes crashing out of the skull and is writ down with glee." Neil proceeds to recall his drug-crazed ravings and violent, irrational gestures on Sunset Beach before a gathering of fellow musicians. His friends tolerate his excessive behaviour after an all-night party as Neil flails in the surf and flashes back to WW II memories of Normandy beach. The narrator then reflects, "I shall one day be free of the ceaseless nagging of invisible ghosts."

Al Neil

Al Neil was born in Vancouver in 1924 at Vancouver General Hospital. He lived near Main and Broadway. At age nine he began classical piano lessons under Glenn Nelson at Quebec Street and 12th Avenue. He graduated from King Edward High School, worked for the Department of Transport as a surveyor and joined the war effort at age eighteen. "What's a guy gonna do? You're naive and there are signs all over the place that say you've got to fight the Huns." In 1944 at twenty he landed on the Normandy beachhead. Returning to Vancouver scathed, he resumed studying piano but soon opted for jazz under the influence of teacher Wilf Wylie and musicians Charlie Parker, Dizzy Gillespie and Bud Powell. Around 1947 he helped establish The Cellar Jazz Club and led the house band, meeting and playing with some of America's most distinguished progressive jazz artists. In the early 1950s he was still working for the post office and living with a wife and two children in Lynn Valley. "But I gave it up," he told one journalist. A second marriage also disbanded. Addicted to heroin, he read extensively and was impressed by writers Rimbaud, Artaud, Breton and

17

Jarry. He also began making collages influenced by the Dadaists and the surrealists.

Much venerated in local print since he assumed residency in a tumble-down waterfront shack without running water in Dollarton (near where Malcolm Lowry lived and drank), Neil has been variously dubbed "one of Vancouver's bona fide underground warriors, a man with a cult following and a hermit's mystique," "keeper of the avant-garde flame" and "a Charlie Parkerish sort of 1960 version of Charles Ives with Schoenberg overtones." His brilliantly inspired or else sadly drunken concerts at the Western Front are semi-legendary. "If you play to the Creator, you don't need an audience," he told *Interface* magazine. "That's the way I've conducted my life. I've never expected anything."

In 1972 the Vancouver Art Gallery hosted a one-man exhibit of Neil's art. His first book, *West Coast Lokas*, was Neil's written accompaniment to the show. He has also released three records, one in collaboration with American poet Kenneth Patchen. Vancouver filmmaker David Rimmer made an appreciative portrait, *Al Neil: A Study*. He continues to give infrequent concerts, infrequent and highly quotable interviews and to sell and exhibit his art, most recently at the Coburg Gallery with Carole Itter in 1985.

His best book, *Changes*, recalls four of fifteen years spent in Vancouver as a junkie and a be-bop musician, from 1958 to 1962. With its many references to sexual experiences, pill-taking, heroin, cheap wine drinking and a graphic description of a visit to the VD clinic, *Changes* appeals with its scatter-brained but highly lucid frankness. It celebrates life a la Henry Miller's *Tropic of Cancer*—it is little concerned with literary conventions and approaches writing as a musician improvises a solo. "This book is a ferrago of funk and feeling," he writes, "butterflies rising from the ashes, thus indicating that further alarming adventures of our hero are about to begin as he plans to measure the circumference of God." *Changes* is easily one of the most interesting underground books of fiction from Vancouver. "I don't mind exposing myself," Neil told Marke Andrews of the *Vancouver Sun*. "I'm completely uninhibited in that respect. A lot of people put that down. They write in the third person. I guess they're afraid to expose themselves."

Pulp Press published a book of Neil's short stories, *Slammer*, in 1982. "Al Neil," says friend and author Brian Fawcett, "gets more pleasure out of walking down the road than other people get from buying a car or skiing down a mountain." Recently endowed with a war pension, Neil continues to live without a telephone on the Dollarton waterfront, commuting to the city to visit friends and to perform.

THIRTEEN

Burrard Bridge

One of the best novels of Vancouver for adventuresome readers is Betty Lambert's *Crossings*, published by Pulp Press in 1979, about the sexual relationship between a man and a woman who repeatedly "cross over," the Burrard Bridge from opposite worlds. Mik, a violent and virile ex-con, crosses over to Vicky's rooming house at 2952 West 8th Avenue. Vicky, a CBC dramatist, crosses over to the coarse but truthful world of Mik and his cronies at the St. Helen's Hotel (currently Theo's) on Granville Street.

Betty Lambert was born in Calgary, Alberta on August 23, 1933. "My father died when I was twelve and I was no longer 'working class,' I was 'welfare class' and I was determined to get out of that class. Writing was a way out but soon it became more than that, it became a necessity." Acutely aware of social injustice, Lambert became a socialist in her teens. She said she used her anger to fuel her art. She moved to Vancouver in 1951 to attend UBC at age eighteen, worked as a copywriter at a local radio station, and graduated to writing radio plays for CBC. Among her plays for children *The Riddle Machine* (1966) was performed at Montreal's Expo in 1967. In her late 20s, Lambert became embroiled in feminist issues which permeated most of her best work for the stage. In 1965 she became a part-time lecturer of English at Simon Fraser University, where she was later made an Associate Professor (with only a BA in Philosophy and English) teaching modern and Greek drama, Shakespeare and linguistics.

Betty Lambert raised one daughter as a single parent and produced approximately sixty plays for radio, television and stage. *Sqrieux-de-Dieu* (Talonbooks, 1975) gained renown as a witty and outlandish sex comedy about a menage a trois. *Jennie's Story* (1983), her most powerful work, was based on a true story from southern Alberta in the 1930s, when a priest had his fifteen-year-old housekeeper, whom he seduced, taken to a mental institution and sterilized. She is told she has had an appendectomy. Later, married and unable to conceive, Jennie learns the truth and commits suicide. *Under the Skin* (1985) is based upon a true Vancouver story of a man kidnapping and sexually abusing a twelve-year-old girl for six months. Lambert won ACTRA's Nellie award for best radio play in 1980 for *Grasshopper Hill*, a drama about a Canadian woman who has an affair with a Jewish survivor of Auschwitz.

Crossings, her only novel, is a penetrating study of female masochism. It is a riveting account of Vicky Ferris' sufferings, mental and physical, with flashbacks to her failed marriage and an illegal abortion in East Vancouver. Unable to extricate herself from Mik O'Brien's influence, Vicky is raped, gets pregnant, demands marriage, discovers the pregnancy alarm was false, retreats to Berkeley, gets pregnant by a stranger and keeps the baby. The skilful clarity of the writing convincingly evokes the protagonist's passion and restlessness. "Maybe it's one huge orgasm, this book. Maybe I just want to remember it once more before I go menopausal. Maybe I just want to feel young again and real and alive. The Victorian era. Repressed lust. But to the girdle do the gods inherit. Down from the waist they are centaurs...Perhaps I shall go mad and run naked down the street at night, waving my bum behind me like a flag. Perhaps I shall leap on beautiful young men, a moustache on my lip. Oh god, it's not fair to grow old. It's not fair. I hate it. I really do."

The book gained the disapproval of one Vancouver feminist bookstore, but its bold truthfulness impressed critics. It was published in the US, with limited success, under the less appropriate title of *Bring Down the Sun*.

Betty Lambert fought a six month battle with cancer in 1983. "In the manner of her death," recalls friend and actor Joy Coghill, "she was absolutely extraordinary. It was one of her greatest gifts to us." Cancer of the lung was spreading through her body. Lambert persevered against the disease valiantly, and dismissed suicide on rational, philosophical and moral grounds. She continued to write, frustrated by lack of time but also impressed with the urgency that the immediate prospect of death brought to her work. "I have so much to do and no time to die," she wrote to Coghill. She composed her own memorial service, including her favourite Gerard Manley Hopkins' poem, "God's Grandeur," to celebrate life.

On August 9th, she completed her final play, *Under the Skin*. In her final days, blind and unable to speak, she enjoyed playing Trivial Pursuit with her sister, Dorothy Beavington. Beavington recalls, "On the night she died she indicated she wanted her yellow writing pad and her pen. She wrote, with much effort, 'Dot, one last trivia question.' I asked Betty if she wanted me to ask her a question and she vigorously pointed to her own chest to indicate *she* was definitely asking me. Then she wrote, 'What is the final demand in life?' I said I didn't know but I was sure that she did. She nodded. Then she slowly wrote her answer, which was, 'More and more and more nostalgia.' "

Lambert was remembered by her colleagues and friends at a Simon Fraser University memorial service on November 21st, 1983, following her death on

November 4, 1983 in Burnaby. SFU subsequently established a playwriting award for SFU students in her honour.

FOURTEEN

Pacific Press

BUILDING, 2250 GRANVILLE STREET

The editor emeritus of Vancouver's major newspaper is Bruce Hutchison, the only British Columbian to have earned three Governor General's Awards.

Bruce Hutchison was born in Ontario in 1901 but grew up in Victoria. He has worked for newspapers since he began as a high school journalist for the *Victoria Times* in 1918. In the 1920s he also wrote pulp fiction, a novel and a film script, "Park Avenue Logger," which was produced in Hollywood. He first worked for the *Sun* in 1938 and served as its editor from 1963 to 1979.

Hutchison's only published novel, *The Hollow Men* (1944), effectively evokes the plight of a BC intellectual who feels alienated from the political centres of power. A political journalist named Leslie Duncan is torn between family life on his father's beloved Cariboo ranch and his professional duties during World War II in Washington, DC and Ottawa ("the counterfeit little world on Parliament Hill"). Nauseated by the intrigue, interminable talk and unalterable weariness of Ottawa and finding himself disillusioned by the staged bravado and empty mythology of America, Duncan strives to be something more than another of "the hollow men" as described in T.S. Eliot's famous poem, from which the novel's title is drawn. He betrays his liberal/Liberal sensibilities to accept a CCF nomination in his home Cariboo riding to satisfy his "appetite for the land" and possibly secure badly needed irrigation for his district. *The Hollow Men*, although overburdened with the representative rhetoric of its namesake, is nonetheless a rare, authentic and valuable work deserving of a wider reputation, especially within British Columbia.

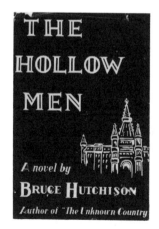

Hutchison is chiefly regarded for his non-fiction books, *The Unknown Country* (1943), a panorama of Canada; *The Fraser* (1950), for the Rivers of America series; *The Incredible Canadians* (1952), a portrait of Mackenzie-King; *Canada's Lonely Neighbour* (1954); *The Struggle for a Border* (1955); *Canada: Tomorrow's Giant* (1957); *Mr. Prime Minister: 1867-1964* (1964); *Western Windows* (1967), a short literary study; the text for the NFB's *Canada: The Year of the Land*; and

21

his autobiography, *The Far Side of the Street* (1976). *The Unfinished Country* (1985) is a companion volume to his first book.

Hutchison's primary allegiance has always been to newspapers and non-fiction ("I was so interested in this business that I never got out, and here I am still in it.") At age eighty he published a second work of fiction, *Uncle Percy's Wonderful Town* (1981), containing nostalgic accounts, through the eyes of a fourteen year old narrator, of life in smalltown "Emerald Vale, BC." Bruce Hutchison lives in Victoria.

Pacific Press is the parent company of the *Vancouver Sun* and the *Province*, both of which are now owned and operated by Southam Inc. Before this monopoly situation existed, the two papers had been fiercely competitive, with the much older *Province* clearly outselling the upstart *Sun*. When the *Province* refused the cooperation of the *Sun* in settling a violent labour strike with the International Typographical Union in 1946, the *Sun* surged ahead to enjoy a roughly 2-to-1 circulation advantage in the 1980s. Formerly, before amalgamation into one building, the two dailies published from the heart of the city, at large buildings near Victory Square. The *Sun* and the *Province* doubled as Vancouver's major book publishers in their earlier years. Many of BC's earlier fiction writers also worked for the *Sun* or the *Province* as journalists.

FIFTEEN

Granville Island Market

Vancouver's most acclaimed author of science fiction is William Gibson, who published a short story, "Winter Market" (*Vancouver Magazine*, November, 1985) which is set around the False Creek area of "Couverville" sometime in the future. "Trashfires gutter in steel canisters around the Market. The snow still falls and kids huddle over the flames like arthritic crows, hopping from foot to foot, wind whipping their dark coats. Up in Fairview's arty slum-tumble, someone's laundry has frozen solid on the line, pink squares of bedsheet standing out against the background dinge and the confusion of satellite dishes and solar panels." The story is narrated by the editor of a newly released album by "Lise," whose creative dreams are marketed like pop songs to achieve instant triple-platinum success. Lise is a doomed "high-tech St. Joan burning for union with that hard-wired Godhead in Hollywood."

William Gibson

William Gibson was born in Conway, South Carolina ("a place like a gas station") on March 17, 1948. He grew up in Virginia and attended boarding school in Arizona. He developed an early interest in the science fiction of Ray Bradbury. At age eighteen, in response to what he calls the "Kafka-esque" possibility of being drafted, he came to live in Toronto's Yorkville district, then travelled in Europe and married in the early 70s. He came to Vancouver in 1972 to be near his wife's parents, graduated from the University of British Columbia, and began writing SF in 1980. In 1981, *Omni* magazine bought the first story he sent, asked for another, and Gibson was encouraged to complete a novel.

His first novel, *Neuromancer* (1984), achieved unprecedented success by winning the Hugo and Nebula Awards for best SF novel of the year, plus the Philip K. Dick Memorial Award for best original SF paperback. Influenced by authors William Burroughs and Robert Stone, as well as musicians Lou Reed and Steely Dan, Gibson wrote what one reviewer described as "a sizzling, computer-age novel, filled with street-Beat poetry and grotty characters from a future underworld where body parts are grown for sale and computer programmers work in 'cyberspace,' an abstract dimension in which software takes on visible shape like neon sculptures." He cites himself as a collage artist who collects computer buzz-words and jargon to mask a slight knowledge of high-tech machinery. He works on a 1937 Royal standard typewriter, referring to writing as "a painful, slow process, like pulling a big chain out of your ear." Gibson sold the screen rights for *Neuromancer* to Hollywood in 1986 for $120,000.

A second novel, *Count Zero* (1986) contains some of *Neuromancer*'s characters and occurs almost a decade later. A collection of short stories is forthcoming. Gibson appeared at Toronto Harbourfront's International Festival of Authors in October of 1985 and explained to one interviewer that science fiction is not essentially about the future. "Science fiction writers who think they are futuristic are naive," he maintains. "Good SF tends to be about aspects of where we are now that we don't like to think about." He lives in Vancouver.

"The States has become as foreign to me as England. I'm very uncomfortable with national identities anyway. The planet is getting smaller all the time, smaller and faster."

Much less highly touted is *Rerun* (1976), a solid SF first novel by Calgary-born **Neil Crichton**, which features a climax in Port Moody. In this bizarre tale, worthy of *The Twilight Zone*, a Port Moody businessman named Charles Johnson is swallowed by a

23

throbbing curtain of light outside his home in 1990. When he unaccountably regains consciousness in an Edmonton hospital bed, twenty-six years old back in 1976, he proceeds to "rerun" his life. Because he knows the future, he can make lucrative business decisions, but the destructive power of ambition ruins his happiness. He desperately hopes to rectify his mistakes in 1990 by hiring a plane which lands in Pitt Meadows. Hoping to re-enter the curtain of light in Port Moody, he is mistaken for a burglar and shot as the light re-swallows him. He wakes in an Edmonton hospital bed, with a teddy bear at his side, in 1956.

SIXTEEN

Granville Island Hotel

PELICAN BAY

A pivotal scene in Bobby Hutchinson's Harlequin Superromance, *Sheltering Bridges* (1984) occurs here when the heroine spots her wealthy romantic interest, Rand Evans, dining with his beautiful blonde ex-wife...who turns out to be a cruel diamond thief.

Bobby Hutchinson is one of a rapidly expanding group of Vancouver romance fiction authors. She was born in Elk Valley, BC on July 29, 1940. She first came to Vancouver in 1958 to be married. "In 1958, if you came from a small town, you either became a nurse or a teacher, or got married." A marathon runner and mother of five, she pursued a career as a freelance writer but was dissatisfied with the low pay. "Then one afternoon I blundered onto a TV show which interviewed Janet Dailey, one of romance's leading writers. By God, she made money. Lots of it. So I got 150 romances and read them, sorted out what I figured I could have fun doing, and spent a year doing it." She sold *Sheltering Bridges* within three months.

Sheltering Bridges is a legitimate novel that evokes emotions and a strong sense of place. When BC government cutbacks force the closure of the Vancouver Private School for the Hearing Impaired (i.e. Jericho School), school director Alana Campbell accepts a proposal from Kootenay mining magnate Rand Evans to tutor his deaf son, Bruce, on a ranch near Fernie. Her virtue is rewarded by marriage, in keeping with the Harlequin formula, after Alana saves Bruce's life during an unbelievable shootout. The aloof Rand then appears at the back of her classroom and proposes to her using the "bridge" of sign language.

"My second romance, *Wherever You Go* (1986) was

a tribute to the Vancouver I love. It had scenes in all my favourite places—the Varsity Grill on 10th Avenue, the Only seafood cafe, the view from behind the Museum of Anthropology. Old men on Skid Row who follow you when you look into their eyes. The sunset on Spanish Banks. Raccoons in the alleys at midnight, swiping garbage. The rain, the city jail, Schwartz' Deli near the Army & Navy. Then Harlequin phoned. They loved it. But could I change the setting to Seattle? I know Margaret Laurence would have hung up the phone in their ear. I said 'No problem.' And so I sacrificed True Art for Mammon.''

Bobby Hutchinson now attracts generous advances for her books and earns a living with them. She is also the author of *Meeting Place* and *Welcome, The Morning.*

"Everybody has the right to fictionalize their own life," says Hutchinson. "Vancouver can pretend just as well as any of us. On a clear summer night, the downtown core, viewed from Spanish Banks, looks serene, regal, floating in the bay like a fanciful city. You have to remind yourself that every shining light in every room is lighting somebody's reality. More often than not, it's not great. It's a bad smelling or petty or vicious reality. Romance is not reality. It's a smoky reflection in a mirror. What you think you see is what you get. And I see the city, floating in the bay.''

Other established romance fiction authors in the Lower Mainland are Frieda Vasilos (*Noon Madness*; *Summer Wine*), Catherine Spencer (*A Lasting Kind of Love*), Caroline Jantz (*Separate Lives*), Christine Hella Cott (*Midnight Magic*; *A Tender Wilderness*; *Dangerous Delight*; *Perfume & Lace*; *Riches To Hold*; *Seaspun Magic*; *Strawberry Kiss*), Moira Tarling (*A Bid For Happiness*; *A Piece Of Forever*), Jo Manning and Elizabeth Graham. Romance agent Mary Novik of North Vancouver co-ordinates an informal support group for romance writers called Pink Ink. Pink Ink hosted a seminar at the Granville Island Hotel in 1985 at which guests learned that thirty-five percent of all paperbacks sold are romances.

SEVENTEEN

1900

WEST 4th AVENUE

Vancouver's most published novelist, Patricia Young, hosted a half-hour radio program for CKMO, the forerunner of CFUN, when the station was located across from the Vancouver Courthouse in 1947.

Patricia Young was born in London, England on June 17, 1923, the fifth of eight children in a poor family. She was crippled by polio at age two. "I started writing about age eight or nine in a clothes closet with a candle. I nearly burned the house down. After that my mother built me a shed in the backyard, which I quickly dubbed 'The Studio,' where I did my writing summer or winter." She published articles in a London newspaper at age thirteen. While working as "a real life Eliza Doolittle" for the Lord Mayor of London at his residence as a secretary, Young, a beautiful blonde, published the first of her twenty-four romance novels with the London firm of Ward Lock, becoming "England's youngest novelist at age seventeen." "I took them my first novel, *Narrow Streets*, in 1942 simply because they were the closest publisher. I didn't hear from them so I stormed into their office one day and demanded my manuscript back. Well, it turned out their letter to me had been bombed. They had a contract there ready for me to sign."

Patricia Young

After writing novels in her family's bomb shelter and being almost fatally injured by a bomb blast, she came to Canada in 1946 on a three month cross-country lecture tour to thank the people of Canada for "Bundles for Britain" that had been sent during the war. Her biggest audience was at the Hotel Vancouver. Liking Vancouver, she decided to stay. She worked for the *Province* for a year during a major strike, then for the James Lovick advertising agency for a year, then for CKMO as she continued to write her novels. She says of her books, "They're the kind of stuff that women go for. I often took a trip somewhere and wrote a book about it to pay for the trip. Once I went up to Bella Coola and wrote a novel but I couldn't sell it. I guess the world wasn't interested in Bella Coola." Her only novel with Vancouver settings is *A Man and His Country* (1953).

Young lived in New York City from 1952 to 1962, writing anonymous liner notes for BMI-RCA Victor. "I was making nothing but money." During this period she researched and eventually published a non-fiction book on religion, *The Prophecy*. As a Catholic who later met the Pope, Young has been researching and writing another non-fiction book since the 1960s, on the Jewish people at the time of Christ. Returning to Vancouver, Young developed an extensive freelance writing career as a syndicated columnist but a brain tumour operation confined her to a wheelchair. She now lives alone in a barren house in a posh neighbourhood, with an enormous oil painting of herself as a debutante over the fireplace. Mementos of her meetings with Bob Hope, Ginger Rogers, Haile Selassie, Winston Churchill, various recording artists,

Mayor Tom Campbell and John Diefenbaker (with whom she corresponded as an unofficial press secretary) are kept amongst her scrapbooks stuffed with newspaper columns and her photo albums. She plans to publish an autobiography called *Reach for the Stars*.

The ashtrays are overflowing cigarette butts marked by red lipstick. She can no longer operate the mimeograph machine in the basement. But she has two more manuscripts she has completed and hopes to publish. "I must have had fifty years of writing. You come to a time when you want to retire. But you never can." Her most recent work is a self-published pamphlet, *The Death Peddlers, Communist China's Opium War on the West* (1973).

(now CALENDERS RESTAURANT), 1540 WEST 2nd AVENUE

In David Gurr's third thriller, *The Action of the Tiger* (1984), John Morris, a part-time English teacher at a Vancouver community college, and his wife, Mary, a recently laid-off nurse at Vancouver General Hospital, share a farewell dinner at Emilio's restaurant, before Mary departs for a year long nursing position in Namibia, South Africa. Mary is kidnapped by terrorists and John must come to the rescue. "I wrote *Tiger* with a Vancouver couple as heroes, thinking I might get a little mileage PR-wise in Vancouver, " says Gurr. "They had a newspaper strike! I am still invisible in Vancouver."

David Gurr was born in London, England on February 5, 1936. He emigrated to Canada in 1947 and came to UBC on a drama scholarship. He served as an officer in the Canadian navy for sixteen years. During a naval visit he met his wife, from Kerrisdale, in the emergency ward of Vancouver General Hospital. He worked as a designer and builder of houses before turning to writing full-time with *Troika* (1979), *A Woman Named Scylla* (1981) and *An American Spy Story* (1984). He lives in Victoria and is preparing an extensive study of Hitler's sex life. "Like Melbourne with Sidney, Vancouver hates Victoria. It is even more insular than Victoria because it can pump itself up with commercial power. It has improved since 1952 but there was a certain charm and naivete to summer evenings on Spanish Banks then. No crusading alderwomen striking down nude males!"

NINETEEN

2249

YORK STREET

The "York Street Commune" was the birthplace of New Star Books, which over the past ten years has generally concentrated on non-fiction. However, included in its fiction list are *Taxi* (1975) and *A Flight of Average Persons* (1979), both by Helen Potrebenko, *In Due Season* (1979) by Christine Van Der Mark, *Soon to be Born* (1980) by Oscar Ryan and *Platonic Love* (1981), a collection of short stories by Scott Watson. New Star has also published a book by Gladys Hindmarch titled *A Birth Account* (1976), which is a record of the author's body sensations, thoughts and feelings during the course of a pregnancy, miscarriage, second pregnancy and birth. New Star Books is also the residence of Vancouver's foremost author of political books about BC, Stan Persky. New Star Books and Persky now operate from a communal house at 2504 York.

Gladys Hindmarch

Stan Persky was born in Chicago, Illinois on January 19, 1941. He served in the American navy from 1958 to 1961, then worked as a warehouseman on the San Francisco waterfront until 1966. He first visited Vancouver in 1964 to do a poetry reading at the New Design Gallery with Jack Spicer and Robin Blaser, who travelled on a Greyhound bus with him and a bottle of brandy. They were guests of Warren and Ellen Tallman; the latter knew Spicer and Blaser from Berkeley. "The first significant person I remember meeting here was Neap Hoover, a possible writer who later became an anthropologist at the provincial museum in Victoria. He was married to Leni Hindmarch, sister of writer Gladys Hindmarch, who was living on the corner of York and Yew. That's how I suppose I first got the idea of living in Kitsilano."

Persky returned to Vancouver with Robin Blaser, now a Simon Fraser University English professor. Persky attended UBC and wrote for the *Georgia Straight*. He received his BA and MA in anthropology/ sociology in 1969 and 1972 respectively. He moved into 2249 York Street in the summer of 1968 and began printing books on a mimeograph in the basement. "This was at first called Georgia Straight Writing Supplement or Vancouver Community Press, eventually turning into New Star Books around 1974 with Lanny Beckman running it. Among the books published in the basement, mostly with Brian DeBeck providing the labour, are Brian Fawcett's *Friends*,

Warren Tallman

George Bowering's *Autobiography* and Fred Wah's *Tree*, Daphne Marlatt's *Rings*, my book *The Day*, plus books by Gerry Gilbert, David Cull, Scott Lawrance, Jorj Heyman, Chuck Carlson and perhaps others.''

Persky shared living quarters with Lanny Beckman, Gladys Hindmarch, her husband Cliff Andstein, their baby son and Brian DeBeck when "York Street West" was established, leaving San Francisco poet George Stanley to operate "York Street East." "George and Angela Bowering camped with us for a while at 2249, and it was also the site of weekly writers' meetings at which George Stanley and I discovered and foisted upon others 'journal writings.' Somewhere in all this we had to make books.''

Persky's first book, *The Day* (1971) is an autobiographical journal/novella seemingly meant to be read aloud to a close circle of friends. "Ten years or so after writing it, I found myself two blocks or so up the street, having decided the world had a surplus of poetry." Persky has mostly taught sociology in Terrace, Nanaimo and North Vancouver and created leftist ripples in political journalism as an author and commentator, producing books of analysis on contemporary issues. *Son of Socred: Has Bill Bennett's Government Gotten BC Moving Again?* (1979) was published to coincide with a provincial election. *The House That Jack Built: Mayor Jack Volrich and Vancouver Politics* (1980) coincided with a civic election. Persky has also subsequently published first hand looks at contemporary Nicaragua, *America, The Last Domino* (1984), and the Solidarity movement in Poland, *At the Lenin Shipyard* (1981). His forthcoming book is a collaborative biographical portrait of NDP Opposition leader, Bob Skelly. His books are all published by New Star.

TWENTY

2305

WEST 5th AVENUE

The birthplace of Harbour Publishing. The house was leased by Max Andersen who ran the once renowned Ectoplasmic Assault light show. He and Howard White bought a Multi 750 press which they operated in the basement, preparing the first issue of White's ongoing magazine of West Coast working class lore *Raincoast Chronicles*, which subsequently prompted White, who moved to Pender Harbour, to operate Harbour Publishing with his wife, Mary.

Howard White was born in Abbotsford on April 18, 1945. His father was a truck driver, jack-of-all trades and gyppo logging operator. White had a logging camp childhood on Nelson Island, BC, taking schooling by correspondence, before the family settled in Pender Harbour. He lived in Vancouver from 1964 to 1969 while attending UBC. Twice winner of Canadian Media Club Awards for best magazine feature article, he won the Eaton's BC Book Award for *Raincoast Chronicles First Five* in 1976. A heavy equipment operator, White's first book of poetry, *The Men There Were Then* (1983), has gained popular favour for its anecdotal tributes to blue collar experiences. In 1983 Pulp Press also released his novelized transcription of tough BC labour leader Bill White's (no relation) outspoken radicalism as head of the Boilermakers and Marine Workers Union. Written in the first person, *A Hard Man To Beat* is a documentary memoir/novel, in the manner of *In Cold Blood* or *The Executioner's Song*, using the raw material of Bill White's "Bareknuckle Bill" persona to create the illusion of an intimate memoir.

"Vancouver is a low-pressure, temperate, medium city," says Howard White. "There's no use talking about its character because it doesn't have one. Its leaders are too self-conscious to allow anything natural and original to happen. If it does, they bulldoze it, as they bulldozed Coal Harbour and False Creek and were barely restrained from bulldozing Chinatown. Their ideas of city-making are all brought pre-fab from Minneapolis, San Diego and Sydney. Or, like the little frogwoman in Stanley Park, from Copenhagen. That attempt to provide Vancouver with an artistic signature tells you a lot about the city. Make us famous all over the world. Except when the city fathers discovered the Little Mermaid had bare breasts, they flew into a puritanical tizzy and ordered their copy sedately bundled into a rubber wet suit. So there she sits, welcoming the world into Vancouver harbour, a piece of bowdlerized imitation, ironically apt.

"I was part of a group called together to discuss possible themes for the BC Pavilion at Expo 86. It was a once-in-a-lifetime experience for a writer. Here were politicians with real power and tens of millions of dollars to spend, suddenly and for the first times in their lives groping with problems that writers spend their days and nights in contemplation of: Who are we? As a community? What is there in our past, our present, our future that distinguishes us? What can we say about ourselves which is not only true, but significant, and striking? Unfortunately, these same officials and generations of their predecessors had previously been so inhospitable to artistic impulses within the community that Vancouver had no Shakespeare, no Dickens, no Jack London, no Mordecai Richler, even, who had put in the necessary lifetimes of thought required to reveal a community's genius, and who now could be turned to for answers. So the officials had to spend their millions on a third-rate amusement park full of statements just as false and embarrassing as the little frogwoman, and Vancouver missed another chance to claim a place in the world.

"Still, as in the case of Canada itself, there are advantages to living in a formless blob, culturally speaking. You can do pretty well anything you want as long as you don't do it in the street and scare the tourists and as long as it doesn't contain economic analysis, political comment or social history—three subjects which have been excluded from receiving any publishing support from the Social Credit government in 1985."

TWENTY-ONE

2862

WEST 22nd AVENUE

Here Keith Maillard lived from 1973 to 1981. The vicinity is most reflected in his first published novel, *Two Strand River* (1976), which he wrote at this address. Kitsilano High School is represented in the book as Sherwood High. A character named Mrs. McKenzie was named after nearby McKenzie Street.

Keith Maillard was born in Wheeling, West Virginia on February 28, 1942. He spent the early 1960s on the road in Florida, New England, New York, Los Angeles, Alaska, Alberta and Nova Scotia. From 1968 to 1970 he was active in the underground press movement, editing a newspaper in Boston. He immigrated to Canada in 1970. He is a musician who produced, arranged and wrote for Vancouver's Ferron in the late 1970s. Active in writers' associations, he is a teacher of creative writing and music. *Alex Driving South* (1980), *The Knife In My Hands* (1981) and *Cutting Through* (1982) are effusive and urgent novels with frequent outbursts of sex and violence, seemingly created from biographical substance matter, in which male protagonists are driven to explore and examine life in the US. In *Alex Driving South*, a CBC producer named Evan Carlyle returns to his native Raysburg, West Virginia to reunite with his volatile high school friend Alex Warner, a suicidal and drunken maniac who drives them across the Mason-Dixon line into the heart of America and dark personal confusions. In *The Knife in My Hands*

31

and *Cutting Through*, a wanderer named John Dupre seeks his family roots and later becomes embroiled in the anti-war movement as a Boston draft dodger.

Two Strand River is an atypical Maillard novel cemented by its narrative structure and thematic formality. In this distinctly West Coast novel about bisexuality, a male protagonist who is an effeminate hairdresser in a unisex salon and a celibate female librarian and former Olympic swimmer literally find one another on the final page, having taken the entire novel to first find themselves. Alan, the hairdresser, learns to obey his transsexual urges to become Alan/Ellen, thanks to a bizarre cleansing ritual on Bowen Island administered by a seemingly conventional middle-aged housewife named Mrs. McKenzie. Leslie, the librarian, retreats with her spartan nature and confused lesbian tendencies to a remote Kwakiutl village where she is referred to as "boy" by an elderly Indian guardian spirit. "It's always there," advises Mrs. McKenzie, taking Alan on a therapeutic journey to the same Kwakiutl retreat, "behind everything. It's male and female...before they were separated...and that's where you are now." The symbolic synthesis of male/female, of Alan and Leslie, is achieved after a bizarre climax of symbolic resurrection at the close of the story which is at odds with the poignant realism that propels the majority of the book. The title is derived from a nursery rhyme.

Maillard's fifth novel, *Motet* (1986) will chronicle the angst of an alternately reckless and inhibited Vancouver pop musician.

TWENTY-TWO

2932

WEST 6th AVENUE

John Gray

This is the fictional address for a communal house of hippie misfits in John Gray's first novel *Dazzled* (1984). This comic satire of counterculture heydays in Vancouver ruthlessly rejects the naive idealism of that bygone era. The protagonist is a failed suit salesman (Gray himself endured the ignoble fate of once working for a prominent local haberdasher) and the climax features a quixotic guerrilla attack on the CBC building.

John Gray was born in Truro, Nova Scotia, in 1947. Now one of Canada's most successful playwrights, he studied theatre at the University of British Columbia and helped form Tamahnous Theatre. His first musical,

18 Wheels, presented the male domain of trucking. Gray, who was named after a deceased flying comrade of his father from World War II, then developed a curiosity about the importance of the great wars on himself and Canada which led him to write, with UBC-reared actor Eric Petersen, *Billy Bishop Goes To War*, a musical which premiered in Vancouver and opened on Broadway in 1980. A third musical, *Rock n' Roll*, based on Gray's membership in a high school rock band, also premiered in Vancouver and has been translated into a television film called *The King of Friday Night*. Although critically panned, John Gray's fourth full-length play to be seen in Vancouver, a comedy-mystery set in Victoria's Empress Hotel at Christmas called *Better Watch Out, Better Not Die*, broke box office records at the Vancouver Playhouse. A children's play for Christmas, *Balthazar and the Mojo Star*, premiered at the Vancouver Centennial Museum.

Gray contributes to *Vancouver Magazine* and is active in politics, spearheading a campaign to ensure that the work and rights of Canada's artists are recognized and protected by the federal government. *Don Messer's Jubilee*, his fifth major play, pays tribute to the populist appeal of the former television program of the same name, for many years the favourite of millions of Canadians. John Gray resides in Vancouver.

TWENTY-THREE

3556

WEST 21st AVENUE

Margaret Laurence

Margaret Laurence, perhaps Canada's most revered novelist, lived primarily at this address during her stay in Vancouver from 1957 to 1962.

"The good things that happened to me there were, among others, my meeting with Ethel Wilson and her great kindness and encouragement to me; the publication of my first novel [*This Side Jordan*] in 1960 and my winning the Beta Sigma Phi First Novel Award for it [in 1961]; my writing of nearly all my West African short stories and also the first draft of *The Stone Angel*, as well as the *The Prophet's Camel Bell*.

Margaret Laurence was born in Neepawa, Manitoba in 1926. Her parents both died when she was young. She was raised by an aunt who had become her stepmother. She worked as a reporter for the *Winnipeg Citizen* and married Jack Laurence, a civil engineer, in

1947. From 1950 to 1957 they lived in Somaliland and Ghana, where her two children were born. Her residency in Vancouver was not an easy one. She separated from her husband in 1962 and moved to England for ten years, divorcing him in 1969. Since 1974 she has made her home in Lakefield, Ontario.

Her first book, *A Tree of Poverty* (1954), was about Somali literature. *This Side Jordan* (1960) was an African-based novel. The fifth book in her Manawaka cycle is *A Bird in the House* (1970), a collection of strongly autobiographical short stories. She has also published books for children, including *Jason's Quest* (1970), *Six Darn Cows* (1979), *The Olden Days Coat* (1979) and *The Christmas Birthday* (1980). The Warner Brothers film version of *A Jest of God*, starring Joanne Woodward, was titled *Rachel, Rachel* (1968).

"I never felt at home in Vancouver, although I admired it a lot and still do. This was not the fault of the city, but rather the fact that, being basically a prairie person, I felt hemmed in between the mountains and the sea, both of which tended to frighten me a bit. People who don't know the prairies quite often feel a similar sense of alienation with the huge expanse of land. I know people from BC and the Atlantic provinces who feel very uneasy if they live a long way from the sea. We are probably formed by our birth-geography more than we know.

"However, Vancouver always figured prominently in my childhood and growing-up imagination. It was the paradise that prairie people ultimately went to, when they retired, usually. It comes into my Canadian writing a lot, of course. Prairie people, when they 'light out' for somewhere else, go west. BC is as far west as we can go. Stacey did, so did Rachel. So, further back, did Hagar. So, later, did Morag."

Hagar, Rachel, Stacey and Morag are heroines from Laurence's acclaimed series of Manawaka novels, *The Stone Angel* (1961), *A Jest of God* (1966), *The Fire-Dwellers* (1969) and *The Diviners* (1974). *The Fire-Dwellers*, in particular, is set in Vancouver.

TWENTY-FOUR

Jericho Beach

Jericho Beach appears as a significant locale in all six volumes of David Watmough's ongoing chronicle of his fictional Cornish-born counterpart, Davey Bryant. Watmough lives nearby and can be seen walking daily along the beach. Especially attentive to nature, he cites the proximity of the Jericho marshlands to his writing desk as a direct inspiration and luxury. "Beyond bobbing mergansers the tall towers stand in stark silhouette while a few yards further I am in the company of muskrats in the marsh and the herons and pheasants make their presence felt through sight or sound. And then there are the familiar faces, some heart-warming, some tragic, wending the narrow paths while often eagles soar overhead. All that, believe it or not, only six or seven minutes from theatre and concert halls. Where else? I ask."

David Watmough was born in London, England on August 17, 1926. He was raised in Cornwall and majored in theology at King's College, University of London. He immigrated to North America in 1952, living in New York and San Francisco. He first came to Vancouver in 1959 on a travel writing assignment for the *San Francisco Examiner*.

"My initial impressions of the place were emphatically negative. Its buildings were mostly nondescript: lots of wooden shacks interspersed with dismal stucco dwellings, calculated, on a rainy day, to turn depression into suicide. The downtown was reminiscent of Boise, Idaho. On a CBC-TV interview about a year later I suggested the place needed an immediate transfusion of 500 Jews and 500 gays. The former might ensure a modicum of cultural growth, the latter improve the ghastly window displays in Woodward's, the Bay and Eaton's. And then came the Vancouver International Festival. It isn't historically accurate, but I date this town's second major march toward cultural maturity from 1960. Vancouver began to move forward out of architectural colonialism about the same time. The fingers of high-rises began to prod the skies in the West End. The contours of a metropolis finally became perceivable. A few natives actually ceased apologizing for everything. Movies opened on Sundays and plans for an arrogant freeway system were frustrated. Only hick mayors prevailed."

David Watmough proceeded to uphold the flag of literature in Vancouver, in both public and in print, with eloquence and serious intent, perhaps more consistently and effectively than any other writer in the past three decades. He developed a far-reaching reputation for "monodramas," delivering hundreds of dramatized readings; he contributed to the CBC and numerous esteemed journals; and most recently he founded the Federation of BC Writers. His major works of fiction are *Ashes for Easter* (1972), *From A Cornish Landscape* (1975), *Love and the Waiting Game* (1975), *No More Into the Garden* (1978), *Unruly Skeletons* (1982) and *Fury* (1984). *Fury*, Watmough's most recent book, is a particularly strong collection of

David Watmough

short stories featuring mature humour, poised sensitivity, heartfelt confessions and the author's fastidious love of musical prose. The best story is an amusing yet disturbing reflection from Davey Bryant after he encounters violence in a Burns Lake beer parlour. "The din of taped rock music was an act of rapine against my Schubert-refined ears." A final story about a chance meeting on windswept Long Beach demonstrates the healing and uplifting quality of Watmough's autobiographical fiction at its best.

In addition, he has produced a study of modern French Catholicism, a book of plays, a record album and a centennial collection of fiction from BC writers entitled *Vancouver Fiction* (Polestar Press, 1985.)

"My change-over to the conviction that Vancouver was not only the city I wished to live in but also to remain in until death us did part was fully established by the mid-1960s. What I found in my adopted city was a corporate state of mind which I quickly grew to admire and strove to embrace—the civic conviction that if you want something accomplished, you do it yourself."

TWENTY-FIVE

3886

WEST 11th AVENUE

Margaret Atwood

Margaret Atwood, one of Canada's foremost writers, lived here in 1964–65, while working as a "lowly lecturer" at UBC. "It was a wonderful breakthrough year for me—in it I finished writing *The Circle Game* and wrote all of the first draft of *The Edible Woman*. I lived in an apartment on top of a house in Point Grey and I had a 180-degree view of the mountains as far as Mount Baker and the harbour and Vancouver Island and it was indeed spectacular. The people who gave me the most support were Jane Rule and Helen Sonthoff, who helped me find an apartment, lent me some of their dishes and a card table, and were in general very hospitable. I must emphasize that at the time I was, of course, not very wealthy. Several of the poems in *The Circle Game* are Vancouver poems and you can probably figure out which ones from the book. I loved the entire year and the only reason I didn't stay was that I felt I had to go back and complete the work for my Ph.D. or I would always be an academic floorscrubber."

Margaret Atwood was born in Ottawa in November of 1939. She has lived and studied throughout North

America and Europe. She is one of Canada's most acclaimed poets, perceptive critics and widely known novelists. Her collections of poetry include *The Circle Game* (1966), *The Journals of Susanna Moodie* (1970), *Power Politics* (1973), *Selected Poems* (1976), *Two-Headed Poems* (1978) and *True Stories* (1981). Her major work of criticism is *Survival: A Thematic Guide to Canadian Literature* (1972). She edited *The New Oxford Book of Canadian Verse in English* (1982) and published short story collections and children's books including *Up in the Tree* (1978) and *Anna's Pet* (with Joyce Barkhouse, 1980). Her novels are *The Edible Woman* (1969), *Surfacing* (1972), *Lady Oracle* (1976), *Life Before Man* (1979), *Bodily Harm* (1981) and *The Handmaid's Tale* (1985).

TWENTY-SIX

4510

WEST 8th AVENUE

Jane Rule

Vancouver's most progressive-minded fiction author, and possibly BC's greatest living fiction writer, Jane Rule, wrote her best-known novel *Desert of the Heart* (1964) at this address. The novel became a feature-length film, *Desert Hearts*, in 1985.

Jane Rule was born in Plainfield, New Jersey on March 28, 1931. Educated mainly in California, she taught for several years in the eastern United States. In 1956, while visiting her family in California, she drove north to Vancouver to scout out an apartment for a friend who had been hired by UBC. As Rule commented in a piece written for *Canadian Writers in 1984* (UBC Press), "There before us was a city of human scale (the only two highrises were BC Hydro and the Vancouver Hotel) defined by thirty miles of accessible beaches and the mountains of the north shore rising abruptly into forest wilderness. As we drove along the tree-lined streets, seeing gardens as lovely as English gardens, then out through the grant lands to a university on cliffs overlooking the sea, I kept wondering why nobody had ever told me of this place, so rarely beautiful, on a coast I'd known nearly all my life. Until that day, that coast had ended for me at Seattle."

She chose to stay in Vancouver where her first job was Assistant Director of UBC's International House during its first year of operation in 1958–59. She taught intermittently in UBC's English Department. Her early BC writing colleagues were Bob Harlow, Phyllis Webb,

Anne Marriott, Marya Fiamengo and CBC producer Bob Patchell. She helped form the Arts Club (before it became a theatre) with Geoffrey Massey, Takao Tanabe, Lawren Harris, John Korner, Jack Shadbolt, Gordon Smith and Arthur Erickson, among others.

"For me, Vancouver was a remarkably rich and nourishing place, and increasingly I felt I belonged there...In British Columbia a dozen cultures mingled uncertainly in small towns isolated by great reaches of wilderness, mountains, deserts, lakes and rivers, and I felt the more a part of it because I was an immigrant too."

Jane Rule's *Desert of the Heart* is a compassionate and unsentimental account of two women who meet and fall in love in Reno, Nevada. A second novel written on West 8th, *This Is Not For You* (1970), takes the form of a letter in which one woman attempts to justify her non-involvement with the woman she loves. While living at 4502 West 2nd Avenue, Rule produced four more books. *Against the Season* (1971) and *The Young in One Another's Arms* (1977) are novels which focus upon difficulties and consolations of people of various ages who try to evolve a sense of community from voluntary relationships. *Themes for Diverse Instruments* (1974) is a collection of short stories. *Lesbian Images* (1975) is a psychological study of twelve female writers.

Rule and former UBC professor Helen Sonthoff moved to Galiano Island where she wrote *Contract with the World* (1980), a novel set in Vancouver. The book is similar to *The Young in One Another's Arms* except the characters are artists from a variety of disciplines. *Inland Passages* (1985) is a major collection of short stories, many of which are set in Vancouver. All twenty-one stories reflect an author who has matured far beyond the mere seeking of praise. Rule is a scrupulously encouraging writer who incites the reader to explore human motives and expand definitions of love with her shrewd perceptions and exacting style.

Rule's sensitivity to the elderly is an important part of her writing. She and Sonthoff are neighbours and close friends with the ninety-year-old painter and author Elisabeth Hopkins. Rule's fiction also effectively captures the manners peculiar to Vancouver. "I have a feeling the kind of dialogue I write is very West Coast. I get an awful lot of flak from eastern editors saying this is absolutely unbelievable dialogue. Their claim is that the only people who are witty are people who use lots of references to books and other intellectual paraphernalia. There's a kind of snobbery in the east, and also a slowness. People are not kindly offhand. There's not the kind of teasing that has nothing to do with anybody needing to be defensive. A sort of joking attentiveness that goes with a more relaxed world."

TWENTY-SEVEN

4170

TRAFALGAR AVENUE

The second most lucrative novel ever written in Vancouver, and possibly the goriest, most distasteful and most sexist piece of writing perpetrated in this city, owes its origins to a friendship dating from the fifth grade at Trafalgar Elementary School in Kitsilano. Jay Clarke and Richard Covell, two of the three authors of *Headhunter* (1985), a thriller published under the pseudonym of Michael Slade, edited the school's newspaper and subsequently studied law together at UBC, where they met *Headhunter*'s third author, John Banks. With the unofficial collaboration of their office assistant Lois McMahon, the three law partners began their eighteen month book-writing project in October of 1981. "We've always enjoyed the brainstorm of bouncing ideas off each other," Clarke says. "Writing the book was just a natural outgrowth of that." The threesome began *Headhunter* after a two-week writing session in the Sylvia Hotel. British publisher W.H. Allen reportedly paid an advance of almost $90,000 for the book. Its cover features the bluish, severed head of a St. Paul's Hospital nurse impaled on a bloodied spear. The story follows the gruesome trail of a psychotic killer beyond Gastown and Grouse Mountain to Seattle, New Orleans and Ecuador. Most of the action occurs in Vancouver. This hair-raising tale of murder, voodoo and sexual slavery is spawning a sequel, but the authors continue to practice law. Clarke and Banks work at 123 Main Street. Covell's office is at 1145 West 7th Avenue.

Michael Slade is the pseudonym for three Vancouver lawyers, **John Banks**, **Jay Clarke** and **Richard Covell**. Clarke was born in Lethbridge, Alberta on May 28, 1947. Banks was born in Regina, Saskatchewan on June 30, 1947. Covell was born in Regina on November 4, 1946.

TWENTY-EIGHT

University Endowment Lands

Eric Nicol

Eric Nicol, Vancouver's most published and best known humourist, has lived in houses within a few blocks of this natural wilderness for most of his life and can still be seen biking "the 16th Avenue freeway" to UBC. He has lived in the same house on West 36th Avenue since 1957 and recalls biking to the UBC Farm as a a student when 26th Avenue was still a mud logging road. His affectionate tribute to this area, "The Swamp," is found in his third book of humour, *Twice Over Lightly* (1953).

Eric Nicol was born in Kingston, Ontario on December 28, 1919. The following year his father moved the family to British Columbia to a small cottage in an orchard on Kingsway in order to accept a job as an accountant with the BC Forest Service. Nicol graduated from UBC in 1941, was with the RCAF as a ground crewman for three years, and returned to UBC to obtain an M.A. in French in 1948. He spent a year at the Sorbonne on a French Government Scholarship, moved to London and wrote radio and TV comedy for the BBC, and began to contribute occasional columns to the *Province*. He returned to Vancouver in 1951 when his column became a permanent fixture in the *Province*. His early work was extremely poised and earned him three Leacock Medals for Humour.

His early humour books include *Sense and Nonsense* (1947), *The Roving I* (1950), *Twice Over Lightly* (1953), and *Shall We Join The Ladies?* (1955). These books went into many printings and encouraged Nicol to try his hand at plays. He became Vancouver's first regularly successful local playwright with *Regulus*, *Like Father Like Fun*, *Pillar of Sand*, several children's plays, and later works. He has also written an excellent history of the city, *Vancouver*, and numerous other books including a sharp satire of Canadian attitudes and government bureaucracy, *Canadide*.

In "Confessions of a Commercial Writer" in the 25th Anniversary Issue of *Canadian Literature*, Nicol asserts with comical finesse that he has been stigmatized as a writer whose work sells. "As a commercial writer I suffer an anxiety attack every time I send an unsolicited manuscript to a publisher or dramaturge, because under Canadian criminal law prostitution is not a crime but soliciting is."

Eric Nicol says his politics are anarchist in theory, liberal in practice. He is nonetheless conservative enough to note that he has no church affiliation and that Vancouver has changed. "Vancouver has lost her heyday some years ago, before the blithe insouciance lost its manners. It is in character for a local to spend the day climbing to the peak of a coastal mountain, and there find a naked person playing the saxophone. What is unseemly is that the incumbent does not invite him to accompany him on his banjo. Not the old Vancouver."

TWENTY-NINE

UBC ENGLISH DEPARTMENT

BUCHANAN BUILDING, UNIVERSITY OF BRITISH COLUMBIA

Vancouver's most ambitious novelist, Cecil Cragg, first joined the faculty in 1946. During his quarter-century at UBC he also reviewed for *Canadian Literature*, the country's first and most significant journal devoted solely to Canadian writing, developed by George Woodcock as an adjunct to the Department in 1959.

Robert Cragg

Robert Cecil Cragg was born in Lethbridge, Alberta on April 2, 1905. When his father went to England to serve as a doctor in World War I, the family moved to a camp north of Portsmouth. At age eleven, Cragg was deeply affected by the sufferings of wounded soldiers, some of whom were returning from the Somme in lorries, having received no previous medical attention prior to their arrival in Portsmouth. From this period he began to wonder, "How the hell do we stop all this nonsense?" Over half a century later he would begin his epic ten-volume novel designed to accomplish that feat: to persuade the world to accept peace.

Cragg was educated in Dorset and Vienna, studied economics for five years at L'Ecole Libre des Sciences Politiques in Paris, and earned three degrees from the University of Toronto, including a doctorate in philosophy. In 1947 he published *Canadian Democracy and the Economic Settlement* and held "left wing liberal" views. From 1949 to 1952 he taught and simultaneously operated a gold mine on the Toulemin River near Hope, BC. He once stood before a disinterested English class holding a $2,000 gold bar. "I got involved in the gold mine by accident," he says. "I'd bought shares and then the president of the company suddenly died. I thought, 'By God, I'll do it.' I had no experience whatsoever but I immediately raised $25,000. But there wasn't enough gold to keep the mine going."

In July of 1971 the retired English professor began to write his projected ten volume, futuristic, political, comic novel about the American-born and orphaned

41

British noble, Eustace Heskam. Writing nearly every day, either at his Point Grey home or at his summer retreat on Lake Cowichan, Cragg finished the series, under the general title of *Sheep May Safely Graze*, on December 4, 1984. After first paying for publication of a separate novel from a female perspective entitled *Brilliant Women* (1982, using a female pseudonym), Cragg made arrangements with Merlin Books in Devon to begin issuing his Eustace Heskam series. The publisher's jacket copy for the first volume, *Caught!* (1983), which was released under the title *Sheep May Safely Graze*, describes the scholarly, musical, boxing champion hero as "a young Hercules in bed and an Apollo on the concert stage." Cragg has since supplied his own jacket write-ups for *Victor of Moscow* (1984), *Talisman* (1984), *Salvage* (1985), *Snow* (1985) and *When Woman is Beautiful* (1986). The volumes yet to be released are *Armful Intimacies*, *No Doubt*, *Practice and Cult* and *Bobbing Buoy*.

"It [the series] is really a comedy," says Cragg, "carried out in a whimsical fashion. You can't change people's minds with heavy satire, or by preaching at people or waving placards." Canada has joined the US, China has muzzled Russia. Europe has consolidated itself. The brilliant Eustace, a sort of globe-trotting intellectual equivalent of James Bond, is unabashedly "all over the map in intellectual pursuits and bodily movements." His fictional mission is to show the reader the future. Although Cragg displays a vast storehouse of knowledge and a dry, bemused wit, it is often difficult to believe the action is set one hundred years into the future and not at Oxford or Eton fifty years ago. Cragg's obtuse references to scholarly matters in his lengthy paragraphs make reading the novels cumbersome, despite plenty of political intrigue and sexual heroics from the irresistible Eustace.

Cragg believes, with his education in the classics and a translation of a French critical study of Shakespeare underway, that readers might enjoy struggling to construe meanings. He once mailed a portion of his grand narrative scope to McClelland & Stewart but the Canadian firm rejected it. He hasn't tried elsewhere. "Canadian literature rather bores me," he says, "because it tries to be so local. And compared to the Americans, we have a very poor literary history. You can name hardly any writers of Canada from the nineteenth century." Collectively, Cragg's handsomely packaged, self-published contribution to global enlightenment represents an unprecedented Quixotic effort that is at once ludicrous and admirable, vainglorious and sublime.

"In a sense, I suppose I'm more of a critic than anything," says Cragg. "As far as being creative, well, I don't know whether I am or not."

THIRTY

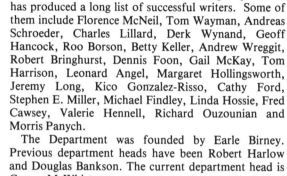 CREATIVE WRITING DEPARTMENT

BUCHANAN BUILDING, UNIVERSITY OF BRITISH COLUMBIA

Canada's first accredited Creative Writing Department has produced a long list of successful writers. Some of them include Florence McNeil, Tom Wayman, Andreas Schroeder, Charles Lillard, Derk Wynand, Geoff Hancock, Roo Borson, Betty Keller, Andrew Wreggit, Robert Bringhurst, Dennis Foon, Gail McKay, Tom Harrison, Leonard Angel, Margaret Hollingsworth, Jeremy Long, Kico Gonzalez-Risso, Cathy Ford, Stephen E. Miller, Michael Findley, Linda Hossie, Fred Cawsey, Valerie Hennell, Richard Ouzounian and Morris Panych.

The Department was founded by Earle Birney. Previous department heads have been Robert Harlow and Douglas Bankson. The current department head is George McWhirter.

George McWhirter was born in Belfast, Northern Ireland on September 26, 1939. He was educated in Belfast and taught high school there until he and his wife immigrated to Vancouver in 1967. He visited Irish hippie friends here in 1966. "When we came here first and I looked at the logs lined up on the beaches, I knew we had enough firewood here to live forever. None of this picking wee bits of coal washed up on stony strands from passing coal colliers that supplied Ireland from the pits in Wales and the North of England. Here there was fat rain and fruit."

McWhirter is a productive but low-profile author of complex poetic writing that features surrealistic flourishes and keen attention to the physical world. *The Catalan Poems* (1971) reflect his experiences of Spain. *Queen of the Sea* (1976) describes the spiritual struggles of a Belfast shipbuilder in a series of connected poems. *Twenty-five* (1978) is poetry about Mexican village life. *The Island Man* (1981) is a book of poems of Vancouver Island where McWhirter lived briefly in 1966. *Fire Before Dark* (1983) contains a fifty-four page poem, "Training In The Language" which evolves from a folk dancing sequence set in Kitsilano's Bayview Community School. It also contains what McWhirter believes to be his best poem, "And Back, And Still By An Early January Morn."

In fiction he has published three diverse and experimental short story collections. *Bodyworks* (1974) is about a mythological character named Hermione. *God's Eye* (1981) contains stories set in Mexico. *Coming To Grips With Lucy* (1982) is stories about

George McWhirter

Irish roots and adaptation to BC. His novel *Paula Lake* (1984) reflects the unique east/west climate of the Pacific Rim with a bizarre, fragmented but compelling storyline. The story opens at Stanley Park's Second Beach where Andrew, a virile lifeguard, falls in love with Paula, an older woman who escorts visiting Japanese students. After making love with Paula in her orderly West End apartment, he decides that a conspiracy of self-control has robbed the visiting Japanese students of their natural selves. As revenge against Paula, he kidnaps one of Paula's surrogate children, a boy named Nao, and takes him to live for a week in rustic isolation at a lake above the Squamish Highway. Andrew tries to explore the possibilities of a wilder, more manly life in touch with deeper instincts but the abduction only leads to a chilling climax of disorientation on a bridge under the surveillance of Paula and the police. The novel is prefaced by a quote from poet Gordon Rogers: "Why do these people, when they have an argument, not come back to see or face you after it? Why do they take off and hide somewhere in the trees? Is that the difference between the people in BC and the rest of us in Canada?" "The BCer," says McWhirter, "is possessed of a furious shyness."

McWhirter claims to have written most of this fascinating novel on a clipboard in his car while waiting for his kids at swim meets. The hero is based upon someone McWhirter knew, "just the kind of boy you would love your daughter to marry except he is ever so muchly fascist."

"It's not about a woman," he continues. "It's really about two adolescents in an adolescent province that refuses to grow up."

"Vancouver to me is, running out to Point Grey, like a fat thumb, and the rest of the province spreads out like the rest of the hand and fingers. It's well padded, sometimes oppressive, but rich and beautiful and substantial to walk on or under. I live in the intellectual-ghetto end."

One example of the many writers the Creative Writing Department has helped produce is **Ann Ireland**, winner of the 1985 Seal First Novel Award. She was born in Toronto on May 19, 1953. She attended UBC from 1972 to 1976. "I look upon those four years as the most formative for me," she says. "That's when changes appeared in leaps and bounds. I wrote in various basement suites, looking out tiny windows to see the grass. Because I went to university in Vancouver I associate it with intellectual/personal awakening. Somehow the timing was perfect and the people I met and became involved with still have resonance. I learned that being an artist meant *doing* it, and not being too concerned with appearing financially success-ful, well-organized and spectacularly clothed (in other words—Toronto). So when I returned to TO I could bring that notion with me and feel (almost) comfortable with it. I found that Vancouver people were very open, eager for new blood, and as artists, utterly individual.''

Ireland's prize-winning novel, *A Certain Mr. Takahashi* (1985), is about the romantic and sexual relations, and eventual rivalry, of two sisters infatuated with a Japanese concert pianist. The sisters return to BC for a family reunion in Victoria, which is described in sophisticated comic relief, and must come to terms with their hidden jealousies regarding Mr. Takahashi. The sisterly rivalry is not dissipated until the close of the novel when the sisters travel to Vancouver to meet Mr. Takahashi signing albums in a Granville Street record store and share an uneventful meal with him and his entourage in Chinatown.

THIRTY-ONE

Freddy Wood Theatre

UNIVERSITY OF BRITISH COLUMBIA

An actress in L.R. Wright's *The Favorite* (1982) is first seen by her future husband while performing in *Dark of the Moon* at the Freddy Wood Theatre. The author herself met her husband after performing in a summer production of *Dark of the Moon* at the nearby Old Auditorium building, prior to the erection of the UBC Theatre Department's present theatre complex.

Laurali "Bunny" Wright

Laurali R. "Bunny" Wright was born in Saskatoon on June 5, 1939. She came to Vancouver in 1949 when her father was put in charge of war assets for western Canada. The family then lived in Winnipeg, Ottawa and Calgary before her father took a teaching job in Abbotsford. "I had a lot of friends in Abbotsford but I felt sort of different," she says. "I made the mistake one day in class of saying I wanted to be a journalist when the teacher asked us all what we wanted to be. I'll never forget it. The whole class stared at me. Somebody even wrote me a note. It said, 'Gernalist. What's that?' ''

When she was seventeen, the family moved to Germany where her father died. She took first year university by correspondence in Vancouver, travelled to Ottawa to study journalism at Carleton, changed her mind, took secretarial courses and landed a job on a weekly newspaper in Mission, BC.

Later, at the *Calgary Herald* she developed her

deliberately unflamboyant style. At a Banff summer writing course under W.O. Mitchell, spurred by her own series of newspaper features on mental health, she began to write *Neighbours* (1979), a novel about a middle-aged woman who gradually goes mad. *Neighbours* won the Alberta First Novelist Award. She says the book was inspired by a remark made to her by a leading psychiatrist, who admitted psychiatry was an art, not a science, and that "none of us know what the hell we are doing."

Her second novel, *The Favorite*, portrays a teenage girl's severe sense of loss after her father's death. Set in Vancouver, the story is loosely drawn from the trauma Wright submerged when her father died almost thirty years before. But the father in the book more closely resembles her husband, and her own two daughters resemble the two daughters. Her third novel, *Among Friends* (1984) is a grey November tale of three Calgary women of various ages whose parallel lives in journalism fail to sufficiently touch. The story superbly captures the black humour of journalists and showcases Wright's ability to expose the intricacies of the commonplace. "Some people have said about that book, well, nothing happens," says Wright. "Other people have really liked it."

Wright found a new American publisher for her fourth novel, *The Suspect* (1985), a murder story set in Sechelt, BC. On the opening pages an eighty-year-old gardener kills his eighty-five-year-old brother-in-law. The only mystery is why. "My mother and my mother-in-law both have groups of friends in which the gossip is much the same as it is amongst my own friends or adolescents," she says. "It occurred to me it doesn't matter how old you get, you stay the same. It follows that people are capable of any action they were capable of as youths. I thought, by God, I bet they're even capable of murder." As another oddly engaging investigation of the commonplace, *The Suspect* drew favourable responses from literary critics and *People* magazine alike. It was awarded the Mystery Writers of America Edgar Allen Poe Award for best mystery novel of 1985. "Sechelt seemed the perfect place for this story to happen," she says. "I wasn't sure how my publisher would react to it in New York. But they were delighted. To people in New York, Sechelt seems exotic." Although *The Suspect* is clearly Wright's most imaginative story to date, in it she is once again examining the degree to which one ought to take or feel responsibility for the duress of others. Cassandra, Sechelt's librarian, has sadly divided allegiances for the elderly murderer and the local cop investigating the case. "It's a good thing in the main, responsibility," Wright writes, "but I have a feeling now that you can carry it too far or get it all wrong."

L.R. Wright resides in Burnaby. Her two daughters, to her pleasure and dismay, are both studying theatre at UBC.

THIRTY-TWO

UBC

FACULTY CLUB, UNIVERSITY OF BRITISH COLUMBIA

Over there. Huddled over a notepad. The short, bearded fellow in the coffee shop. That's Ian Slater, one of Vancouver's most accomplished novelists, at work on another eco-thriller. "When I'm writing I prefer non-specific background murmur or silence. Much of my writing has been done in the reading room and the coffee shop of the Faculty Club. I use a pencil and eraser for my first draft. This horrifies the computer aficionados but so far they haven't made a word processor that I know of that you can use in a coffee shop."

Ian Slater was born in Australia on December 1, 1941. He worked for the Australian Navy and Australian Department of External Affairs and as a marine geology technician for the Oceanographic Institute in Wellington, New Zealand. He came to Vancouver in 1966 to work for the Institute of Oceanography at UBC. He gained his doctorate in political science from UBC in 1977 with a thesis on George Orwell. He teaches Interdisciplinary Studies at UBC.

Ian Slater

Ian Slater's *Firespill* (1977) illustrates the dangers of tanker traffic on the Pacific coastline by realistically depicting a tragic collision between a Russian tanker loaded with high octane and an American tanker loaded with crude oil, thereby setting two thousand square miles of ocean area on fire. *Sea Gold* (1979), featuring the adventures of a UBC oceanographer who sails from Vancouver's Ballantine Pier, depicts the desperate struggles between Canadian entrepreneurs and multinational claim jumpers for precious metals discovered on the sea floor. *Air Glow Red* (1981) reveals the potential dangers of microwave radiation and international confrontation inherent in the "Star Wars" plan of the US to place deadly weaponry in space. "I'm leery of being a shrill environmentalist. My only point is that when you have technology you have to be careful with it. Technology misused or going wrong is what interests me," says Slater, who says he has seen the film *Dr. Strangelove* so many times that he knows every line of dialogue.

In addition, Slater's comprehensive critical study, *Orwell, The Road To Airstrip One* (1985), has earned extensive critical praise. "It is doubtful," wrote the reviewer in the *Washington Post*, "that any book provides a better foundation for a full understanding of Orwell's unique and troubling vision."

Of Vancouver, Slater says, "The natural beauty of Vancouver is undoubtedly an attraction. The most serious deficiency is the lack of first rate newspapers and magazines of comment like Britain's *Spectator*. There are some good columnists, like Ilya Gerol and Jim Taylor, but alone they can't fill the yawning gap. As for book reviewing here, it's a desert. The book review editors, instead of believing in local talent, prefer to feed off American wire services, not because they are better, only because it's cheaper."

THIRTY-THREE

Mary Bollert Hall

UNIVERSITY OF BRITISH COLUMBIA

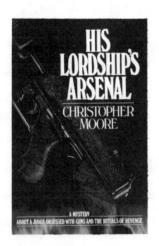

The protagonist of Christopher Moore's first novel, *His Lordship's Arsenal* (1985) is a Vancouver judge who recounts his youth and education at the UBC Law School in the early 1950s when the Dean's office was a converted army officer's bedroom "in what looked like a working-class brothel," Mary Bolton Hall. "Not the sort of place where you'd stumble over a table of Nobel Prize winners." The protagonist Matthew Burlock recounts a bizarre family history of involvement in the international gun trade and connects his exotic past with his investigation of a grisly double murder in Vancouver's run-down Delrose Hotel.

Christopher Moore was born July 8, 1946 in Lincoln, Nebraska. Educated at Oxford, he taught law at UBC for ten years. "I first visited Vancouver in the spring of 1974 for an interview. Most of the interviewing occurred in the Faculty Club. Lawyers have this obsession about eating food. Whether you use your fingers, where you put cherry stones, whether you can tell which fork to use first, and whether you call a laundered piece of cloth a napkin or serviette. I guess they liked the way I ate."

In Vancouver he was active in ACTRA and the Federation of BC Writers while producing radio plays such as *Sticks and Pucks* set in the Canucks' locker room, *The Semi-Detached Barrister* set in the West End and *The Bamboo Pillar* set on Powell Street. He credits screenwriter and playwright Michael Mercer with teaching him the science of dealing with CBC staff changes, David Watmough with teaching the Zen of decision making, Phil Savath and Rich Drew for teaching that the ancestral chart of independent television producers begins with the shark, and playwright Tom Cone (whom he never knew personally) for teaching that "to get noticed in Vancouver you should move to New York."

Moore now lives in New York where he pursues a writing career full time. "When I think of Vancouver I think of tree-lined streets, stucco houses, well-maintained gardens, mountains, forest and the sea. The sort of place which makes people from Toronto, especially in the winter, feel very insecure. Everything works, is swept, polished and healthy. And when you mention the *Times* people assume you mean London and not New York; an intellectual trait which deserves full marks...My favourite Vancouver literary location is Wreck Beach and the abandoned World War II gun towers. How many universities have nude beaches protected by high rise bunkers on their doorstep? Students would be beating down the door to get into that university, but Wreck Beach is a well-kept secret. In the case of an invasion, and you are naked, this is a good place to hide."

The two Wreck Beach gun towers north of the law school have inspired other writers as well as Moore. A crazed Vietnam vet in Christopher Hyde's thriller, *The Wave* (1979), forewarns the RCMP of an explosion at the Mica Dam with a phone call from UBC. "If you require proof of my actions, you can check the parking lot above Wreck Beach. I will be waiting below in the gun tower by the sea."

Described in the *New York Times Book Review* as "an all too graphic picture of a possible catastrophe," *The Wave* is about an American scientist, Jonathan Kane, who struggles to counteract a conspiracy to destroy the Mica Dam and thereby collapse a downstream nuclear plant on the Columbia River, unleashing a radioactive wall 745 feet high, drowning cities, crippling the economy of the western United States and turning the Pacific Ocean into a dead sea.

Written despite an understandable lack of cooperation from the BC Hydro Authority but based upon extensive research, *The Wave* also features a conscientious CBC journalist named Halleran. Before Halleran is killed, he comments, "The whole Columbia thing was put together when W.A.C. Bennett was running the province. Wacky didn't give a buffalo chip about the Columbia Project...But you Americans were offering a lot of money for the Columbia, and Wacky wasn't the type to walk away from a dollar...Wacky took the money and signed the treaty. A few years later the chickens came home to roost and he actually had to build the dams...By the time he finished the dams, they'd cost four times what he'd paid for them."

Christopher Hyde wrote *The Wave* on the strength of his experiences in Vancouver as a CBC public affairs reporter. He now lives in Ottawa, where his brother has also become a bestselling adventure novelist.

THIRTY-FOUR

Musqueam Indian Reserve

6370 SALISH ROAD

The village of "Longstrand" in Crawford Kilian's novel of coastal tribal life in 2703, *Eyas* (1982) is located at the site of the Musqueam Band's reserve.

Crawford Kilian was born on February 7, 1941 in New York City. He grew up in Los Angeles and Mexico. He worked as a technical writer and editor for the Lawrence Radiation Laboratory in Berkeley prior to immigrating to Vancouver in 1967. He became a Canadian citizen in 1973 after studying Canadian literature at Simon Fraser University. He first taught English at Vancouver City College in 1967. In 1968 he began teaching at Capilano College where he has been Coordinator of the Communications Department since 1975. Throughout the 1980s he has been a trustee of the North Vancouver School Board. He contributes articles on education to the *Province* and resides in North Vancouver's Deep Cove area, originally attracted there by "Lowry country."

In 1978 he published *Go Do Some Great Thing: The Black Pioneers of British Columbia* and a sci-fi novel, *The Empire of Time*. His first disaster novel, *Icequake* (1979) is set in Antarctica and was widely distributed. A second natural disaster novel, *Tsunami* (1983), is about the world-wide chaos caused by a West Coast tidal wave that destroys San Francisco, where most of the action occurs, but spares Vancouver. His most original novel is *Eyas*, a fantasy adventure story that imagines a post-glacial period when local civilization is slowly reviving after millenia of barbarism. Eyas, the sensitive leader of The People, must combat his childhood friend, Brightspear, heir to the Sunns who want to dominate the coast with military power. The Goddess of the People is a whale who can communicate telepathically with her naked subjects. The spiritually sophisticated followers of Eyas and the mechanically sophisticated followers of Brightspear must clash in a struggle that has a precedent in the culture clash between Pacific Northwest Indians and the first Europeans here.

"At some point it would be fun to do a pair of novels about Vancouver, one dealing with its origins and growth and the other describing its destruction. The city's springing into life as a 'high-tech' town of the 1880s, complete with telephones, and its growth into a miniature metropolis on the edge of an enormous wilderness, make it a potent symbol.

"I'm surprised that more writers haven't exploited this city as a setting and a metaphor. It was the biggest sawmill town in the world in the 1960s; now, thanks less to our own efforts than to the upheavals that have wracked the rest of the world, we are a cosmopolitan city of refugees who have by incredible luck reached this good place when our countrymen have died in the South China Sea, or the streets of Hue, or the police cells of Chile and Argentina, or a dozen other nightmares. I think we cherish Vancouver all the more because we know how different it is from most of the rest of the world, and how easily it could be swept away."

THIRTY-FIVE

Marshlands

SOUTH OF SOUTHWEST MARINE DRIVE

This is a favoured haunt of bird watchers and "quite possibly the most civilized man in Canada," George Woodcock, who lives in nearby Kerrisdale. Although Woodcock has published minimal fiction, he has written over fifty books and is possibly Vancouver's most important literary figure.

George Woodcock was born in Winnipeg on May 18, 1912. His father, a keen bookman, wished to name his son George Meredith Woodcock, after the English novelist George Meredith. His mother objected— Woodcock has no middle name. When Canada proved economically inhospitable, mother and son returned to England in 1913. In poor health, his father followed, and found work as a railway clerk. Woodcock grew up poor, outside London. "No birthday parties were given me lest children from better-off homes should tell their parents how poorly we lived," he writes in his autobiography.

As a child, he read voraciously and hated sports. "From learning to play alone, I came to prefer working on my own, relying on myself as I have done ever since." He excelled at, but loathed "the guerrilla war between boys and masters" and claims school gave him "the negative gift of a sense of time." His summers in Shropshire with his paternal grandparents were a comparative Eden and gave birth to his lifelong appreciation of nature and poetry. When his father died of Bright's disease in 1927, Woodcock retreated further into the world of books. A guilt-ridden relationship with his self-sacrificing mother pains him still. "Devotion to the father, hostility to the mother, if I fitted into Freud's oedipal patterns, it was in a strange and backhanded way. And if, as I suspect, the theory that our creativity flowers from emotional wounds is correct, then there is more than coincidence to the fact that my development as a poet coincided with the most painful stages of my relationship with my mother."

A well-to-do grandfather offered Woodcock funds for university with the proviso that George study to become an Anglican minister. He declined the offer and was forced into eleven dreary years as a clerk for the Great Western Railway. Infrequent trips to Wales stirred his spirits. In 1930, alone in a railway carriage with a socialist volume of William Morris on his lap, Woodcock realized it was time to sink his personal grievances against his parsimonious grandfather into "the great pool of wrong done to all the oppressed and unfortunate." Drawn to leftist idealism, Woodcock overcame his shyness to hobnob in Bohemian haunts, begin the first of three unpublished novels and publish his first collection of poems, *The White Island* (1940).

In 1940, Woodcock also formed a free-thinking journal, *Now*, which lasted until 1947. Over the years George Woodcock, as an editor, was to publish or befriend such legendary figures as George Orwell, Dylan Thomas, T.S. Eliot, Lawrence Durrell, E.M. Forster, Henry Miller, e.e. cummings, Stephen Spender, Herbert Read and Alex Comfort. He has written books about George Orwell, Herbert Read, Malcolm Lowry, Thomas Merton, Gabriel Dumont, Aldous Huxley, Amor de Cosmos, Gandhi, Henry Walter Bates, Pierre-Joseph Proudhon, Peter Kropotkin and William Godwin. During World War II, Woodcock applied for exemption from military duty conditional on his doing farm work, served the war effort as a labourer, met a twenty-two-year-old anarchist, Marie Louise Berneri (still an inspiration over thirty years after her death), and married his present wife Inge in 1943. In 1944 he also published his first book of prose, *Anarchy or Chaos*.

After the war Woodcock led a hand-to-mouth life as a book reviewer and editor, befriending George Orwell after an initial feud, and publishing his first biography, *William Godwin: A Biographical Study* (1946) and his first literary study, *The Incomparable Aphra* (1948) about England's first female professional writer, Aphra Behn. But Canada began to beckon. "One [reason] was the personal myth which told me that Canada was the real home to which I must one day return, the place where I could perhaps live out some of my father's unlived life. The other was the feeling akin to claustrophobia that by the end of the war...even Britain seemed an island too small to be endured.''

Drawn by the Christian anarchist idealism of the Doukhobors and encouraged by his correspondence with Doukhobor Pete Maloff, Woodcock and his wife arrived to homestead on Vancouver Island at Sooke in 1949. This first half of his life is recorded in his partial autobiography, *Letters to the Past* (1982). When efforts at small-scale farming failed, Woodcock was unable to secure teaching positions at any Canadian university because he had never attended university. He shovelled manure for seventy-five cents an hour, received a Guggenheim grant and went to teach at the University of Western Washington. Refusing to renounce his anarchist views a year later, Woodcock was denied re-entry into the US whereupon Earle Birney helped him secure a teaching position at UBC. He published his first book about Canada, *Ravens and Prophets: An Account of Journeys in British Columbia, Alberta and Southern Alaska* (1952) and became the first editor of *Canadian Literature*, an influential quarterly he steered until 1977. Relations between Woodcock and the university have not been entirely without friction over the years. In 1963, Woodcock resigned his professorship after being denied a request for unpaid leave, and more recently, in the 1980s, Woodcock and UBC have had quarrelsome relations concerning the amount the university is willing to pay for purchase of Woodcock's substantial private papers.

"A British Columbian by choice, a Canadian by birth," Woodcock has twice refused the Order of Canada (on the grounds that it comes from the state) but he accepted a Governor General's Award (from his peers) for his study of George Orwell, *The Crystal Spirit* (1966). Since then he has written or edited over fifty more books. He has been variously dubbed "a great human being, protean and in some understated way, magnificent," "a kind of John Stuart Mill of dedication to intellectual excellence and the cause of human liberty," "a man of avid curiosity and intelligence trying to come to terms with his times," "an unswerving individualist," "a romantic idealist," and, by his English schoolmates, "Timberprick." Politically he can be termed a pacifist anarchist.

In a 1977 essay about British Columbia politics, Woodcock claimed the Lower Mainland fosters "a uniquely hedonistic existence, the renowned lotus life on the shores of the Gulf of Georgia." The typical British Columbian, he goes on to state, "no matter how gregarious he may seem, sees himself dramatically as a loner in a world of loners." As a result of these two factors, he believes British Columbians are especially susceptible to "the kind of politics that ends in a cult of people rather than of classes." Successful political leaders in BC, he concludes, will be those who recognize the need "to mirror the British Columbian's personal myth of himself as at once a loner and a good man of the people."

THIRTY-SIX

Metro Theatre

1370 SOUTHWEST MARINE DRIVE

DR. LAURENCE J. PETER
Author of *The Peter Principle*

THE PETER PYRAMID

OR, WILL WE
EVER GET THE POINT?
ILLUSTRATED BY MATT WUERKER

The best selling non-fiction book ever written in Vancouver owes its birth to an unsuccessful production at this theatre. The late Raymond Hull, as a member of the audience, retreated to the bar and happened to mention his dissatisfaction to a stranger. The stranger was Laurence J. Peter. He agreed the production was not successful. He then advanced his personal theory that invariably people tend to rise to their level of incompetence and then remain there. Hull thought this was an interesting idea. He told Peter he would like to continue their conversation at the next intermission. The two men shared Peter's "incompetence theory" as to why things go wrong in any hierarchy until Hull suggested they get together to discuss writing a book about Peter's idea. That book became *The Peter Principle* (1969). *The Peter Principle* has sold millions of copies worldwide and has been translated into twenty languages.

The Peter Principle was named after Laurence Peter (and was not called the Hull Principle due mainly to the benefits of alliteration. Hull happily conceded the title is also catchy because there is an underlying soft-core porn connotation to the wording).

With the success of *The Peter Principle*, Laurence Peter moved to southern California to pursue an career as a novelist. "When I met him," recalled Raymond Hull, "he was teaching at UBC. We did no more collaborations after his departure, because the way we worked involved sitting down, face-to-face, and talking over each point in detail. Obviously this could not be done by correspondence." Raymond Hull remained in Vancouver, publishing a wide variety of non-fiction and how-to books that include *Writing for Money in Canada* (1969), *Gastown's Gassy Jack* (1971, written with Olga Ruskin), *Vancouver's Past* (1974, written with Gordon and Christine Soules), *The Male*

Climacteric (1975, with Helmut Ruebsaat, MD), *How to Get What You Want* (1979) and *How to Write How-To Books and Articles* (1981). His adapted stage play, *The Drunkard*, is often performed.

Raymond Hull was born in Shaftsbury, Dorsetshire, UK on February 27, 1919. He immigrated to Canada and Vancouver in 1947. "As I rode in the bus towards Vancouver, a well-meaning man in the next seat said, 'It's a tough seaport town, boy! Keep your hand on your money.' The town is tough, indeed! Only a little below the surface is a thriving underworld of crime and vice. Yet, if one can stay clear of that, Vancouver is a stimulating place to live. A large part of the population—at least of the segment I've known—consists of people who have pulled up stakes and moved here, looking for something better, freer, more exciting than what they knew at home. These are people bursting with ambition, buoyed up by hopes, spouting out ideas, plans, dreams, determined to make something, do something, be something different, new, daring, unconventional! Mixing with people like this, how could I not be stimulated?

"The physical growth of the city has inspired me, too. I knew the West End as a nest of old wooden rooming houses; I see it now, an area of tall apartments—many of them elegant, some positively beautiful. I saw the city constantly smothered in smoke from the umpteen thousand wood, coal and sawdust burning furnaces; I see it now, most of the year, with atmosphere sparkling clear. I've seen the development of mini-parks, big parks, fountains, beautiful public patios and gardens, handsome bridges, and much, much more. I'm not trying to write a guidebook to the city...I'm describing the effect of such changes upon me. They convince me that we, as human beings, do have the power to beautify our environment, and to improve our own lives."

Raymond Hull died at St. Paul's hospital on June 8, 1985. A wake was held at the Vancouver Press Club.

THIRTY-SEVEN

Vancouver College

5400 CARTIER STREET

The model for "St. John's College" in *The Last Sunrise* (1984), a US-published mass market paperback novel co-authored by Norman Carelius and Verna Kidd of Nelson, BC, is Vancouver College.

Norman Carelius was born in Montreal on October

28, 1941. **Verna Kidd** was born in Salmo, BC on April 19, 1939. As writing partners, they scouted locations for *The Last Sunrise* in Vancouver to make their story of two Pacific Rim trading families, one Japanese and one British Columbian, as authentic as possible. The Shaughnessy mansion called "Drachenschlucht," for example, is based upon a house on Angus Drive. As a novel of romance and bi-cultural business intrigue, *The Last Sunrise* tries to strike a balance between popular entertainment and credible evocations of Vancouver and Japan. "My grandfather spent twenty-five years in the Orient," says Carelius, "and was involved in the silk trade. I have his books and pictures from the 1920s. Also, our real life friend, Hiro Kasai, was the model for our fictional Hiro Takazawa. Mr. Kasai is a martial arts expert and a zen practitioner. He also lives in Nelson." *The Last Sunrise* involves the education of Hiro Takazawa's son at Vancouver's "St. John's College." It is an ambitious novel, spanning generations and continents, which has drawn minimal Canadian recognition due to its packaging and American publication.

THIRTY-EIGHT

St. George's

SCHOOL, 3851 WEST 29TH AVENUE

Sheila Watson, author of what has been called "the first truly modern Canadian novel," *The Double Hook*, attended university here for two years when the premises were operated as the Convent of the Sacred Heart.

Sheila Watson was born in New Westminster in 1909. Her father, Dr. Charles Edward Doherty, was superintendent of the Provincial Mental Hospital so the family lived on the grounds of the Riverview institution. She was educated at the Sister of Sainte Anne in New Westminster (77 Albert Crescent) before starting university at the Convent of the Sacred Heart and completing her Bachelor and Master of Arts degrees at UBC in the early 1930s. She taught school at various BC locales and passed two years in the Cariboo region where, she says, "I sank roots I have never been able to disentangle." In 1941 she married poet Wilfrid Watson, a professor of English at the University of Alberta. They moved to Toronto where both taught and Sheila Watson began to write about the Cariboo region. She lectured at UBC from 1948 to 1950 and taught in Powell River the following year. Her first short story

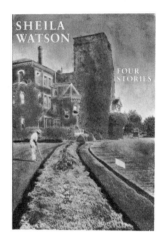

appeared in 1954. During two years in Calgary she wrote her celebrated novel, *The Double Hook*, based on her stay in Dog Creek as a teacher in 1935-37.

The Double Hook (1959) is a short, complex, symbolic novel about the dynamics of a small unnamed interior BC community. A son murders a powerful matriarch at the outset and the various characters of the settlement must adjust to an altered and revitalized cohesiveness. Rich in poetic imagery, biblical echoes and moments of stark realism, *The Double Hook* has garnered a lasting reputation as a major stepping stone in the development of Canadian literature. Only Elizabeth Smart's *By Grand Central Station I Sat Down and Wept* (written in Pender Harbour, BC) has earned such widespread praise for such a slim and singular accomplishment. The precision and austerity of Watson's sophisticated narrative reflects an original anti-naturalism and boldness that continues to make *The Double Hook* one of the most popular experimental novels ever written in Canada. Originally titled *Deep Hollow Creek*, the novel consciously avoids regionalism but nonetheless expresses the quality of rural life unique to the dry Cariboo region. A collection of fiction, *Four Stories*, was published in 1979.

Watson completed her doctoral dissertation on Wyndham Lewis, under the direction of Marshall McLuhan, in 1965, taught at the University of Alberta from 1961 to 1975, and retired with her husband, Wilfred, to Nanaimo. The couple founded a small literary magazine, *White Pelican* (1971-78).

Wilfred Watson's family emigrated from England in 1926 to Duncan, where he attended high school. His first collection of poetry, *Friday's Child* (1955) won a Governor General's Award. He remains active as a painter and writer.

THIRTY-NINE

Morris'

SECOND-HAND STORE, 4394 MAIN STREET

For many of his years in Vancouver, the late D.M. Fraser lived in the apartment above the store. The apartment was dubbed the Vancouver Least Cultural Centre (a parody of the Vancouver East Cultural Centre, a popular venue for theatre and music). Fraser's friends often gathered for private literary readings in his apartment. There were at one time two fridges, one with a Do Not Open sign because it was full of fruit flies. When playwright Tom Walmsley came to stay with Fraser—and therefore drink with Fraser—he went into the kitchen after an all-day binge to find something to eat. The story goes that Walmsley searched the bare cupboards until he opened one cupboard and, in his inebriated state, believed that he saw snakes leaping towards him. The snakes were potatoes that had been left to go to seed for several months, sprouting elaborate twisted white vines.

Donald Murray Fraser was born in New Glasgow, Nova Scotia in 1946. He was the only son of a Presbyterian minister and a high school English teacher, both of Scottish descent. His parents encouraged his precocious reading habits and expected him to become a university professor. Fraser attended high school primarily in Glace Bay and came west to UBC on a go-anywhere scholarship. "I was a coward," he said. "This was the furthest away I could get and still stay in Canada." At UBC he met his future publisher Stephen Osborne, one of the primary founders of Pulp Press, who published D.M. Fraser's critically acclaimed collection of short stories *Class Warfare* in 1974. "I decided writing and working at Pulp Press was a lot more interesting than working with academics," Fraser said.

D.M. Fraser

D.M. Fraser became a semi-legendary, semi-underground figure—the brilliant alcoholic writer who squandered his genius in seedy bars and late-night sentimental reveries. He once described his private life as very small potatoes in the greater scheme of things and was sensitive about his reputation for a self-described dilapidated lifestyle. "I resent that. I'm not Bukowski. It gets in the way. Whenever anything about my personal life becomes an impediment to what the words say, then I get annoyed. I don't care what anyone thinks of me personally, but I do care what people think of my writing. If that stuff sets up a smokescreen then I may as well not write. Read what the books say. Don't worry about what I do in my spare time. When I die I'll let you know."

He made annual pilgrimages to Glace Bay and liked to imagine that he might one day establish an outlet for Pulp Press in Nova Scotia. "I regard myself as a Nova Scotian in exile," he said. The "small boy with the big ears and the precocious vocabulary" in one of his *Class Warfare* stories had grown into an urbane, rabbit of a man who uniquely combined critical mindedness with an extreme passivity and tolerance. "I have always maintained," he said, "that anyone is entitled to believe in anything as long as that belief is guaranteed ineffectual," the cause assuredly lost." Pulp Press published a second collection of stories and elaborately improvised essays, *The Voice of Emma Sachs* in 1983, once more to unanimous critical acclaim. Reared to be reserved and reticent, Fraser only became a man of action in print, bursting forth his undeniable genius with one of the most astonishing prose styles in Canadian literature.

D.M. Fraser succumbed to a lung infection, a complication of pneumonia, at Vancouver General Hospital on March 4th, 1985. He reputedly made several attempts to flee the hospital before being forcibly detained with sedatives. After a memorial service at the Kearney Funeral Parlour, literary acquaintances gathered at the home of Steve Osborne and Mary Beth Knechtel. There, Bob Mercer, editor and instigator of D.M. Fraser's short-lived column in the *Georgia Straight*, recalled the day he attended a Solidarity rally at Empire Stadium and spotted D.M. Fraser seated by himself high up in the bleachers. Thinking they could join Fraser and escape the hokey sentimentality of an Irish band endeavouring to lead the crowd in a rousing version of "We Shall Overcome," Mercer and his wife went and sat on either side of Fraser. But Fraser, well-known for his slurred speech and soft voice, stood up and began to unabashedly belt out the song, causing Mercer and his wife to join him. "And you know Don," recalled Mercer. "Of course he knew all the words."

Class Warfare and *The Voice of Emma Sachs* are works of extraordinary genius. They rank with the finest works of Malcolm Lowry and Hubert Evans as some of the most splendid literary achievements that British Columbia can offer. Although some work by D.M. Fraser will likely appear posthumously, his loss is both maddening and saddening to those who could distinguish the dense clarity of his unique style of writing and his poised, submerged sensitivity in person.

"I can't be intolerant of what I love," he said, "but what I love doesn't necessarily conform to my ideas. My ideas are the intellectual part that got trained to observe and judge. That was what the education was for. That part of me is still very much extant. But it has nothing to do with what I will enjoy and from whom and why. It could be a constant battle except I don't regard it as a battle; I regard it as a constant sort of play, a tension...This self-analysis makes me nervous...But the society in which I grew up was repressive psychologically. I was taught to keep my feelings to myself. To be reserved and reticent. There are periods when you can overcome it and there are periods when it closes in and you think, my god, I'm giving too much away here. But writing, that's what it's for. You have to give it away."

FORTY

Jewish Community Centre

OAKRIDGE, 950 W. 41st AVENUE

Not, at a cursory glance, a hotbed of literary activity, Oakridge is the central area for Vancouver Jewish culture and, as such, supports writing with well-attended readings and seminars at the Jewish Community Centre. Oakridge is the setting for several short stories in Terry Gould's first book, *How the Blind Make Love* (1984), published by Dona Sturmanis' short-lived Orca Sound Publishing at Cambie and Hastings in Gastown. "Oakridge is my 'Little Flatbush,' " says Gould. "It has a heavy concentration of East European immigrant-types and their children's children to which I can easily relate; all with irrepressible outlooks. For some reason this enclave is thought not to exist in Vancouver but it certainly does."

Terry Gould was born in Brooklyn, New York on June 30, 1949. He first visited Vancouver in 1970 during "the great urban-expatriate, Vietnam migration" in his search for a "topographical cure for neurosis." Now a member of the Writers' Union of Canada, Gould and his family have successfully homesteaded in a log house near Telkwa, BC, where he is completing a novel. "Coming from where I do— Brooklyn, not northern BC—I can only see Vancouver as a playpen filled with safely ensconced innocents, who garner a good deal of vicarious cosmopolitan pleasure by bragging about their town's 'crime rate' and 'high level of street prostitution.' But who minds this kind of indulgence? Not me. Set in space amidst snowy mountains and sea, Vancouver is one of those rare cities you can see out of, from anywhere in town; get out of in less than half an hour; or be indubitably a part of—in any one of its distinct, trim quarters: the West End and English Bay; Downtown (which has always reminded me of a clean and beautiful woman with a kinky side to her that can, under appropriate circumstances, be expressed tastefully); Kits, Point Grey; even untouchably rich Langara.

"I have been around the world twice—above the Equator and below—and nowhere else have I encountered such a delightful place to dine out, ride buses, look at ladies' legs, dance—even live and *work*! A midnight stroll can be taken amidst hookers as innocuously pretty as the daytime mountains; past punks you can be sure are only playing at degeneracy— feeling all the while ninety-nine per cent confident of arriving at your destination safely; or, if you are held up by one of Vancouver's half dozen thieves, knowing he will at least say 'please.' Well, what can I say? Compared with Brooklyn or Berlin, Vancouver makes me wax hyperbolic!''

FORTY-ONE

1375

NANTON AVENUE

George Godwin, who wrote what can best be described as The Great Fraser Valley Novel, *The Eternal Forest* (1929) lived at this address while employed for many years at the Canadian Bank of Commerce.

George Godwin was born, probably in England, in 1889. His first book, *Columbia, or the Future of Canada* (1928), was published in a prestigious British series of social commentary and analysis. "In England," Godwin warned the armchair imperialists, "there is a widespread belief in an aggressively British Canada... The truth is, Canada has long since become Americanized... Today, this province is sentimentally British, economically American." Godwin discussed the possibility of BC's union with America and remarked, the Canadian "reads American fiction because Canada has so far produced only the Muscular-Christianity School a la Ralph Connor and a handful of third-rate Cowboy-Cum-Sourdough novelists."

The Eternal Forest realistically depicts the erosion of rural, community-based life in the valley by Vancouver-based capitalism. "Under the effulgent sunshine of the warm Pacific Slope, pessimism wilts and perishes. It is the land of the optimist, of the speculator, of the get-rich-quick merchant, of the booster... and now has come Vancouver, young, raw, unsophisticated, arrogant, like a lad newly in long pants, conscious of departed childhood, deceived by budding virility into belief in its maturity." The circle of characters includes a remittance man Bob England, a parsimonious Old Man Dunn who dreams of returning to England, Lulu who flees to Vancouver to deliver an illegitimate still-born child, her virile but shy Norweigan beau Kurt and a couple only identified throughout as the newcomers.

Rich in empathy and controlled insights, *The Eternal Forest* nonetheless unapologetically translates the anti-Oriental biases of its period. At first the newcomer refuses to sell "to a Jap or a Chink or any other sort of Oriental." Eventually he is driven to Vancouver where he finds the grandson of The Settlement's Scottish founder working comfortably as a realtor, contemptuous of agrarian life. "Sure, I'm out for the dollar," says the realtor. "Why not? Ain't everybody out for all he can get? You bet yer!" The newcomer reluctantly lists his land for sale. At the novel's end he returns at night to "the immemorable bush that had ceded for a time a little to that parasite man, watching, incurious and patient, the birth of the city and its growth. The eternal forest that would witness in the fullness of the city's passing, its decadence and death; the forest, invincible and cruel, that would claim back its own and stand triumphant at the last, rooted fast in the shattered masonry of a forgotten city."

In 1930 Godwin published *Why Stay We Here?* and the first comprehensive biography of the Anglo-Dutch explorer, Captain George Vancouver, simply titled *Vancouver, A Life*.

The only other novel to attempt to broadly fictionalize the early settlement patterns of the Lower Mainland, David Corcoran's *The West Coasters* (1986), has the packaging and elements of a drugstore "adventure epic." Opening in 1857, the Michener-styled "sweeping saga" has a wide ethnic range of fictional characters and historical figures. Governor James Douglas, Amor de Cosmos and Gassy Jack Deighton share the tale with a homeless Nootka mother named Sitka, a Chinese widow named Mei-fu who opens the first brothel, a villainous timber merchant named Cains and a rival, honest timber merchant named Galer. The unification of the colonies and the Great Fire are incorporated amongst depictions of scheming, boozing, political corruption, genteel British manners, Chinese labourers and lonely woodsmen.

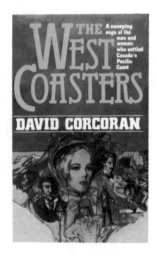

The prose of *The West Coasters* is mostly as uncreative as the title, but the author does a superb job weaving the characters' fates and balancing the emphasis between male and female perspectives. As well, some of Corcoran's fanciful rationales for major historical shifts are intriguingly possible and his extensive research material is skillfully included. **David Corcoran** was born in Toronto in 1953, educated at UBC in the Fine Arts and Creative Writing Departments, was editor of *Prism International* and edits the Vancouver Community Arts Council's *Arts Vancouver* magazine. He plans to continue *The West Coasters* saga in future books.

A third novel of early Vancouver life, Marion Crook's self-published *A Question of Justice—1886* (1986), follows a school teacher heroine as she uncovers a gun smuggling plot to help Metis rebels. The story includes anti-Oriental rioting, dull dialogue, a murder and basic analysis of social development. Like *The West Coasters*, this tale also culminates in the Great Fire. **Marion Crook** was born in 1941. She has self-published five previous BC mysteries from her home in Williams Lake. She has recently secured distribution for her titles from a major trade publishing house.

FORTY-TWO

967

WEST 10th AVENUE

Isabel Ecclestone Mackay

This was the primary address of early Vancouver's major female novelist, Isabel Ecclestone Mackay in the 1920s. In the previous decade she lived at 1656 Pendrell Street and 1034 Denman Street. Her homes were important meeting places for the writers of her time.

Isabel Ecclestone Mackay (nee Macpherson) was born on November 25, 1875 in Woodstock, Ontario. In 1895 she married Peter J. Mackay and in 1909 they moved to Vancouver where she wrote her major works. An active socialite, she was first president of the Canadian Women's Press Club and president of the BC section of the Canadian Authors Association. She corresponded with writers such as Pauline Johnson, Bliss Carman, Charles G.D. Roberts and Duncan Campbell Scott. In 1911, to help raise funds to finance Pauline Johnson's *Legends of Vancouver*, Mackay read Pauline Johnson's poetry to an influential gathering at the Pender Auditorium. An executrix of Johnson's will, Mrs. Mackay was rewarded for her loyal friendship with the bequeathment of "three of my smaller toilet pieces, videlicet: my shoe-horn, my nailfile, and my tooth-brush handle." Mackay's poetry books, *Between the Lights* (1904), *The Shining Ship* (1918), *Fires of Driftwood* (1922) and the posthumously published *The Complete Poems* (1930) exhibit a flair for the melodramatic poesy popularized by Pauline Johnson. Although Mackay could be ingratiatingly self-deprecating in her letters, her published prose is less affected than her poetry, for which she received high praise during her day. Poetry, at that time, was very much "the thing to do," so her superior talents as a novelist have been overshadowed by her reputation as a poet.

Her first novel, partially set in Vancouver, was *The House of Windows* (1912), a comic tale of good intentions and skulduggery gone awry following the innocent adoption of an abandoned baby by a department store clerk and her blind sister. *Up the Hill and Over* (1917) and *Mist of Morning* (1919) were followed by *The Window-Gazer* (1921), also partially set in Vancouver, a discreet tale of a woman's slowly increasing affections for a chronically distracted professor. Her final and best novel, *Blencarrow* (1926) is about a small Gaelic community in Woodstock and the love of three men for one woman. I.E. Mackay died on August 15, 1928. More poetry, *Indian Nights* (1930), was also published posthumously.

FORTY-THREE

954

WEST 7th AVENUE

At this location once stood a venerable, three-storey communal house both famous and notorious for sheltering as many as six well-known Canadian writers and their ancillary lovers at the same time. Andreas Schroeder recalls "the house on West Seventh" and its heydays before one of the above-mentioned lovers chose to leave her plastic purse on the gas heater in the first floor living room and almost torched an entire page from BC's literary index.

"The sidings had been painted a vigorous purple, the window frames flat black, the balustrades and railings fake woodgrain, and despite all this our unfazeable landlord (who, honest to God, really *did* drive a pink Cadillac) continued to allow us $20 off the already cheap monthly rent for the 'maintenance costs' we ran up with all this painting. Inside, the *piece de resistance* was the living room, which had been wallpapered with 300 leftover posters from a promotional drive for my literary magazine *Contemporary Literature in Translation*—posters featuring a curvy silkscreened nude whose 300 sets of trompe d'oeil eyes followed one around the room so insistently that people excessively drugged or drunk routinely lost their nerve and hid underneath the furniture. (What a nude with trompe d'oeil eyes had to do with literature was never formally established, but it was generally held that if you had to ask about it, you were from the wrong century.) The house was considered by both its inhabitants and the professors and students of UBC's Creative Writing Department to be the department's unofficial Annex, and was used for the better part of four years for virtually all departmental parties and bashes.

"The residence roster, from about 1968-1971, included J. Michael Yates, writer/professor; John

Skapski, poet; Charles Lillard, poet; Eric Forrer, writer/adventurer; St. John Simmons, poet; Richard Ward, playwright; Roy Starrs, journalist; David Frith, poet; Ed Clyne, SF writer; Rudiger Krause, German poet; Wayne Stedingh, poet/editor; and myself. Perennial found-ins included George Payerle, poet/novelist; Susan Musgrave, poet; Marci Nori, poet; Ken Belford, poet; Pat Lane, poet; Derk Wynand, poet/professor; Hannah Van der Kamp, poet; Paul Green, poet; Ian Whitehouse, poet; George McWhirter, poet/professor; Michael Finlay, poet/radio journalist; Valerie Hennel, poet/producer; George Amabile, poet/professor; George Porkolab, radio producer; Stanley Cooperman, poet/professor; Fred Cawsey, songwriter/TV journalist and others whose names I'll remember just after it's too late.

"Probably the house's greatest asset was its library. We were all incorrigible book buyers, book traders, even (a few) book stealers, and the result was the most wide-ranging library east of the UBC Main. No matter what book you needed, at whatever time of day, all you had to do was to position yourself in the house's stairwell and holler out *Homo Ludens*! or whatever—it was almost guaranteed to come sailing down from one of the upper floors or flying up from below.

"And the typewriters clacked and tickered and dinged away twenty-four hours a day—especially through the night. No matter how early or late you came home, there was always one or another body banging away on his Smith Corona. We got tanked, stoned, screwed, mad and exasperated, we talked and argued for days on end, conducted musical jam sessions that lasted entire weekends, took full loads of courses and worked every freelance end toward the middle for the rent, and yet I have never written or read as much per year as I did in those days, not even when I geared up to full-time writing, which I have now been doing since 1975.

"There were at least a dozen books written in that house, probably more, but the titles I recall include John Skapski's *In the Meshes* (poetry); Michael Yates' *The Abstract Beast* (fictions), *Great Bear Lake Meditations* (poetry) and *Man in the Glass Octopus*; Charles Lillard's *Cultus Coulee* (poetry); Wayne Stedingh's *From a Bell Tower* (poetry); David Frith's *The Plastic Undergrowth* (poetry); and my own *The Late Man* (modern parables), *File of Uncertainties* (poetry) and *The Ozone Minotaur* (poetry).

"Two magazines were launched in that house, the *Canadian Fiction Magazine* under the editorship of Wayne Stedingh and Janie Kennon, and my own *Contemporary Literature in Translation* (co-edited with Michael Yates). A number of anthologies were assembled there, *Volox: Poetry from the Minor*

Languages of Canada and *Contemporary Poetry of British Columbia*, and even a literary press: Michael Yates' Sono Nis Press. I wrote half a dozen radio plays in my digs on the second floor (beside that single bathroom) and assembled at least a dozen hour-long radio documentaries for the CBC; also two filmscripts which made celluloid (*The Late Man* and *The Theft*) and several hundreds of feature stories, book reviews and columns for the *Vancouver Province*'s *Spotlight Magazine*.

"The house overlooked the present-day Expo 86 site across what was then a smear of grimy, abandoned or about-to-be-abandoned industrial sites—old sawmills, warehouses and loading docks—but when the morning sun touched the waters of False Creek, around 5:30 a.m., it was as beautiful as if it had been Dollarton beach or the Indian Arm. I can't begin to count the times I stayed up for that sun, after a long night's writing, pushing myself just long enough to see False Creek turn to high-voltage platinum and then falling onto my mattress for the day's four-hour sleep. We even had a genuine sea-hag for a neighbour on our west side, Ludmilla Birkenstock yclept, who appears in my current work-in-progress, a micro-novel called *The Mere End of the Finger*."

Andreas Schroeder was born in Hoheneggelsen, Germany on November 26, 1946. He emigrated with his parents in 1951. He developed his interest in European surrealism at UBC where he studied creative writing under J. Michael Yates and Michael Bullock. He founded and edited *The Journal of Contemporary Literature in Translation* (1968-80), contributed a literary column to the *Province* (1968-73) and was the first BC chairman of the Writers' Union of Canada (1976-77). A screenwriter and translator, Schroeder has published several works of poetry, a collection of short fiction called *The Late Man* (1972) and is best known for his superb non-fiction account of his eight-month incarceration (Oakalla Maximum Security Prison, Haney Correctional Centre, Pine Ridge Camp and Stave Lake Camp) for possession of four pounds of hashish, entitled *Shaking it Rough* (1976).

"Prison is *not* a face-off between long rows of malicious, sadistic uniformed guerrillas on the one side," he wrote, "and an equal length of deranged, slavering mother-raping murderers on the other. That may be how the two sides choose to see each other, but the true picture is much obscurer and sadder than that. Prison is a huge lightless room filled with hundreds of blind, groping men, perplexed and apprehensive and certain that the world is full of nothing but their enemies, at whom they must flail and kick each time they brush against them in the dark."

Schroeder's best and most ambitious work is an

Andreas Schroeder

incredible documentary-styled novel, *Dustship Glory* (1986), based on the true story of a dirt-poor Finnish-Canadian farmer in Saskatchewan named Tom Sukanen who began to build an ocean-going, small freighter in 1931. After enduring seven years of gruelling toil and ridicule, his dustbowl ark was completed. Then came the hard part. He was fifteen miles from the closest river, 1027 miles from the nearest salt water. Sukanen began to haul the "Sontianen" (a Finnish word meaning dung beetle) with only the aid of a ploughhorse and a dead-man winch. In three years he had pulled the ship four miles. During World War II, exhausted and penniless, this stubborn mechanical genius was incarcerated in an insane asylum where he died in 1943.

Schroeder, himself an accomplished carpenter (he built the house he lives in in Mission, BC), researched Sukanen and then expanded the already bizarre story into myth. The result is one of the most remarkable novels ever written by a British Columbian.

FORTY-FOUR

Writers' Union

3102 MAIN STREET (HERITAGE HALL)

One of the many writers involved with the Writers' Union of BC is **Joan Haggerty**, born April 26, 1940 in Vancouver. After graduating from UBC in 1962, she used her training in theatre and English to teach drama in London, England. She later published a book about teaching unruly primary school children in London's East End, *Please Miss, Can I Play God?* (1966).

Haggerty's first novel, *Daughters of the Moon* (1971), as its title suggests, is about the struggles and rewards inherent in femininity. Two women, Sarah and Anna, meet and become lovers on the Spanish island of Forementera, during their pregnancies. Anna's husband commits suicide in Paris. Sarah has left her husband in London. Anna dies in childbirth. The novel culminates in Sarah's delivery of a girl. The book is divided into nine sections; the style is late-60s, exploratory and often fragmented.

Joan Haggerty lives in Vancouver and has taught Creative Writing at UBC.

There are many other organizations in which writers are involved in Vancouver. Some of these include: the Federation of BC Writers, Rm. 126, 736 Granville; West Coast Women and Words, 640 W. Broadway; the

League of Canadian Poets, c/o 15097 Victoria Ave., White Rock; the Periodical Writers' Association of Canada, Ste. 209, 402 W. Pender; Vancouver Industrial Writers' Union, c/o 1160 Burrard; Kootenay School of Writing, #105, 1045 W. Broadway; Writers' Guild of ACTRA, #911, 525 Seymour; Playwrights' Union of Canada, New Play Centre, 1512 Anderson; Canadian Authors' Association, c/o #1704, 2045 Nelson; and the Alcuin Society, c/o C-6, RR #1, Bowen Island, BC. 1622 W. 7th Avenue houses several organizations, including the Association of Book Publishers of BC, the Canadian Book Information Centre and the BC Book Prizes. The Booksellers Association of BC can be located c/o Blackberry Books, 2206 W. 4th, and the BC Library Association is at PO Box 35187, Stn. E, Vancouver. The Burnaby Writers' Society is at 6450 Gilpin Street, Burnaby, and the Sechelt Writers' Festival can be contacted at RR #1 Sandy Hook, Sechelt, BC V0N 3A0.

FORTY-FIVE

Intermedia Press

4 WEST 7th AVENUE

Gabriel Szohner

Now primarily a printing company, Intermedia was a major producer of local literature, mostly poetry, in the 1970s, when Intermedia was headquartered on Beach Avenue at Hornby Street. Besides their own work, poets Ed Varney and Henry Rappaport, who still manage Intermedia, published several works of prose fiction such as an anthology edited by Paul Belserene, Michel Tremblay's *Stories for Late Night Drinkers* (which earned UBC's Michael Bullock the 1978 Canada Council Translation Award) and one novel by a local writer, Gabriel Szohner's *The Immigrant* (1977).

Gabriel Szohner was born in Hungary in 1936. He arrived in Canada in 1957 and first published short stories in Hungarian-Canadian newspapers. With the sponsorship of Margaret Atwood, P.K. Page and James Reaney, he was awarded a Canada Council grant to complete *The Immigrant*, an unsophisticated first person narrative of a Hungarian's adaptation to his new life in an unnamed BC interior town, from July to Christmas. The immigrant has a sensitive interior but a rough exterior. He is drawn to an illicit, reckless and secretive affair with his married landlady, Kitty. He sometimes pities himself for not being a native Canadian in the face of racial prejudice and given the conduct of his violent and uncouth fellow Hungarian labourers. Immature, hateful and haunted by flash-backs to domestic and social turmoil during Hungary's revolution, the narrator ultimately loses Kitty and drunkenly considers his immigrant's plight in the snow outside a church on Christmas Eve. *The Immigrant* is Gabriel Szohner's only major publication in English. He lives in Vancouver.

Norman Frizzle, born in Middleton, Nova Scotia in 1946, wrote the other novel-length fiction, self-financed and produced by Intermedia, *The Rape of Mozart* (1973). It's a freewheeling memoir by a twenty-year-old Vancouverite from Ontario, who discovered at age sixteen that he was the centre of time. The narrator has schizophrenic and homosexual tendencies and a juve-nile Messiah complex. The title is derived from a CBC radio interview with the narrator in 1971 in which the narrator claims that Mozart died in 1941. It ranks as one of the worst novels in Vancouver literary history.

FORTY-SIX

1945

KITCHENER STREET

This was the principle address of Vancouver's first resident novelist, **Augusta MacLennan**. While living in Fort Langley, serving as the community's second teacher, she wrote and self-published *Love's Divine Alchemy* (1893), a story of North Carolina during the height of the slavery era. Her second novel was called *Snatched from Neptune's Bosom*. MacLennan's burial place is not known. As an American who outlived her husband, Augusta MacLennan likely returned to the United States.

Whereas colonial writers like MacLennan more often than not feel obliged to write of foreign places in foreign times for foreign readerships, the younger breed of fiction writers in BC invariably is writing to translate the here and now. "I haven't written a book, and I can't think of one I will write, that doesn't have some flavour of some of my city in it," says **Frances Duncan**, born in Vancouver on January 24, 1942. "We moved every year until I was twenty and except for five years back east, all moves were in Vancouver." One of Duncan's short stories, "Was that Malcolm Lowry?," in *Vancouver Short Stories*, published by UBC Press in 1985, recalls her residence as a child in the Dollarton area of North Vancouver.

Duncan graduated with an MA in Clinical Psychology from UBC in 1963 and then worked as a psychologist for ten years before turning to writing. Her first adult novel, *Dragonhunt* (1981) is a short, surrealistic, feminist tale of mythic pretensions, set primarily in Boundary Bay at the Canada/US border. Sir George Werthy, a 700-year-old, door-to-door knife sharpener arrives and slaughters the pet goat of the protagonist, Bernice Carswell. She homesteads on Galiano Island where Sir George is killed while slaying a dragon. Bernice experiences a surreal resurrection through drowning and clam digging.

Her second adult work, *Finding Home* (1982) and two juvenile novels, *Kap-Sung Ferris* (1977) and *The Toothpaste Genie* (1981) are set in Kerrisdale and Point Grey. Her first published work was historical fiction for juveniles, *Cariboo Runaway* (1976).

Politically, Duncan sees Vancouver "being the business end of a province settled by resource rapists, and their beleaguering legacy to the arts." Spiritually, she recognizes Vancouver not at the end of the country but rather at "the entrance to another medium." Nostalgically, she remembers "cutting Christmas trees in the Endowment Lands when everyone knew what *saltchuck* meant."

FORTY-SEVEN

Old Europe

RESTAURANT, 1608 COMMERCIAL DRIVE

Brian Fawcett

"I used to think the centre of Vancouver was at York and Yew," says Brian Fawcett. "In those days half the writers in Vancouver were living in a three or four block square area. Now, for me, it's Commercial Drive, say between First Avenue and Venables. Most of us live over here. The Old Europe is a good place to find writers. I do my revisions there. You can go there at one o'clock and sit all afternoon with a cup of coffee. And Friday nights all the writers go to Santo's. It's a Portuguese restaurant right across from Continental Billiards."

Brian Fawcett was born in Prince George, BC on May 13, 1944. His father was forced to sell the family's ice cream plant when a large dairy corporation instigated' a policy of eradicating competition. On forestry survey crews for the Peace River Dam project, Fawcett witnessed the falsification of forestry reports to allow for the area to be flooded without first being logged. As he became increasingly aware that the lives of people in the BC interior were being controlled by economic decisions from outsiders, his disenchantment with the political status quo and his desire to investigate alternatives led him to Vancouver in 1965. "In direct terms, I came down because I could no longer get what I needed to develop as a writer from Prince George. I needed people to talk to and university. And I'd read everything in the goddamn public library up there. I'd had it. I couldn't live in Prince George."

In Vancouver he attended Simon Fraser University and became enamoured of Tish poetics and left wing politics. He founded a small magazine called *NMFG* (No Money From Government) and published seven books of poetry. "I grew tired of the horrible seriousness of poetry. I came off as the most serious poet in human history. In fact, the way I am and the way I see the world is not terribly serious. I'm a joker. I began to question why I was writing poetry. There's absolutely no audience for it. We live in a country that has created an amateur poetry. It's amateur in that it makes no attempt to come to terms with its readership. It has destroyed its own audience."

Fawcett had a dream which changed his writing career. He dreamed he was a poet who skated poorly but nonetheless received a tryout with the floundering Toronto Maple Leafs. He transcribed his dream on his new Apple computer, embellishing it only slightly, and realized he had written a remarkably entertaining short story. His first collection of stories, *My Career with the Leafs and Other Stories*, published by Talonbooks in 1982, mined his memories of boyhood in Prince George. His second collection, *Capital Tales* (Talonbooks, 1984), packaged his diverse experiments with storytelling and continued his explorations of violence. "A lot of my stories begin with the fact of violence," he says. "You try to discover where the violence came from and where it leads to. I grew up in a very violent environment. I think I understand violence instinctively. I spent most of my youth avoiding punches thrown at my head."

The Secret Journal of Alexander MacKenzie (and Other Stories) (Talonbooks, 1985) is his most ambitious, coherent and powerful collection. Beginning with a title story which fictionalizes the journal of Alexander MacKenzie to symbolize the birth of European exploitation in the BC hinterlands, the often comic stories identify our common enemy as the global village concept.

Fawcett is clearly a resistance writer against the invasionary forces of the 7-Eleven culture, often waving his hands in the reader's face with the facts and opinions of an impassioned essayist, but matching his serious intent with colourful caricatures, fanciful narrative twists and wry wit. He see the book as a fictionalized history of the northwest part of Canada outside the urban areas.

"I see the country that I grew up in as being in essentially the same position as the Republican Army in Spain during the Civil War. The people who live there who ought to be in charge aren't, and they're losing. They're being defeated."

Fawcett teaches writing to prisoners and works as a planner for the Metropolitan Planning Commission. "When I moved to Vancouver I figured I wanted to find out how this goddamn economy works. I realized I wasn't going to do that by going to CPC-ML (Communist Party of Canada—Marxist-Leninist) meetings. I was going to find out by actually working inside the structure of government." He takes pride in the role he played in a resident-based development plan for Bowen Island on behalf of the Greater Vancouver Regional District. "I used to see the city as a series of opportunities that I had to sample. Now increasingly I go to specific places. It has something to do with just getting older but it's also because I understand cities better. They're not simply middle class opportunities." As a professional planner no longer loyal to any specific political ideology, he sees himself as a "situationalist" in terms of his approach to problem solving.

"By this time I know a lot about Vancouver. The way the political system works and where the sewage treatment plants are. I think people ought to know where the water supply comes from, where the poop is going. I'm fascinated by water pipes. Always have been."

FORTY-EIGHT

Octopus Books

1146 COMMERCIAL DRIVE

Juils Comeault

Juils Comeault and P.R. Brown opened Octopus Books on W. 4th Avenue on April 1, 1977. Both this bookstore and the one on Commercial Drive (known as Octopus East) have since become an important meeting place for local writers to pick up new and second hand books and to read from their works.

Comeault was committed to providing a forum for writers and was an enthusiastic supporter of readings for local poets and prose authors. Some of the many readers at both the west and east stores have included Roy Kiyooka, Jon Furberg, Helen Potrebenko, Cathy Ford, Carole Itter, Al Neil, Scott Watson, Gerry Gilbert, Billy Little, George Stanley, Norm Sibum,

Florence McNeil, Carolyn Zonailo, Joanne Yamaguchi, Avron Hoffman, bp Nichol, Bill Schermbrucker, Betsy Warland, George Bowering, Gary Geddes and Mark Warrior. Comeault also organized a playwrights reading series with Tom Cone. The store has also hosted many book launchings by local publishers, including a book of short stories by women, *Common Ground*, published in 1980 by Press Gang.

Juils Comeault died in November, 1983. The bookstore remains an important supporter of local literature.

The most important private collector of local literature in the first half of the century was **Frederic William Howay**, born near London, Ontario on November 25, 1867. His family moved to Clinton, BC in 1870 and to New Westminster in 1874. In 1884 he taught school at Canoe Pass near Ladner, then moved to Boundary Bay School in 1887. With his lifelong friend, Robie Reid, he entered Dalhousie Law School in 1890 where two graduating classmates were future premiers of BC, Richard McBride and W.J. Bowser. He was admitted to the BC Bar in 1891, opened a joint practice with Reid in 1893, was narrowly defeated as a Liberal candidate in the 1906 provincial election and was appointed New Westminster County Court judge in 1907. With E.O.S. Scholefield he published a two volume history of BC, *British Columbia from Earliest Times* (1914), which remained the standard reference text for many decades. His breadth of scholarly curiousity extended to historical sites, place names, journals of early coastal explorers, book reviewing, collecting pamphlets and books and publishing hundreds of historical articles. He edited numerous books and also published *British Columbia, the Making of a Province* (1928) and *Builders of the West* (1929).

Howay received many honours as BC's most active regional scholar, culminating in his election as president of the Royal Society of Canada in 1941. He was also a UBC senator from 1915 to 1942, a New Westminster school trustee, first chairman of the New Westminster library and a recipient of the King's Silver Jubilee Medal. He retired from the bench in 1937. As chairman of the Historical Sites and Monuments Board of Canada, he became especially engaged in the erection of commemorative cairns. He died in New Westminster on October 4, 1943. Notification of his election as a Fellow of the American Geographical Society was received after his death. A bronze plaque in his memory was placed at the Clarkson Street entrance to the New Westminster Courthouse on November 26, 1943. His private collection of local literature was donated to UBC where it remains a major contribution to the UBC Special Collections library.

FORTY-NINE

Burnaby Arts Centre

DEER LAKE PARK, 6450 GILPIN, BURNABY

Fantasy author Eileen Kernaghan launched her career as a paperback novelist when her first science fiction story, "Starcult," appeared in *Galaxy* magazine in 1971, inspired by the offbeat history of the Arts Centre in which Kernaghan has worked since 1967. Originally used by the two pioneer families and as a Benedictine monastery, the building became headquarters for the flamboyant and self-styled Archbishop William Franklin Wolsey of the Temple of the More Abundant Life, until Wolsey departed—in some haste—to California in 1967. As Arts Council Coordinator, Kernaghan used an office that was formerly the Archbishop's kitchen. She developed an interest in charismatic religious leaders of Wolsey's ilk. As a member of the Burnaby Writers' Society ("A more solid support group I can't imagine") Kernaghan developed her interest into her first published story.

Influenced by the works of Evangeline Walton, Ursula K. LeGuin, Tanith Lee, Elizabeth Lynn and Henry Treete, Kernaghan took seven years to write her first sword 'n sorcery fantasy novel, *Journey to Aprilioth* (1980), about a lost civilization and a seeker named Nhiall. "Pre-history is like salt peanuts," she says. "Once you get into it, you can't stop. A sorcerer, for me, is far more interesting than someone who is into biofeedback." Her other novel, *Songs from the Drowned Lands* (1983) earned the Canadian Science Fiction and Fantasy Award. A sequel to conclude her trilogy will feature Bronze Age warriors, earth-magic and the building of Stonehenge in Wessex, circa 2,000 BC.

Eileen Kernaghan was born in Grindrod, BC on January 6, 1939. "My experience as an axe-warrior is minimal," she has noted. She came to Vancouver to attend UBC in 1956 and has lived here, with brief interruptions, ever since.

"On my suburban corner in South Burnaby we have a West Indian spice shop, an East Indian grocery, a Chinese convenience store, a Danish bakery, an English fish 'n chips shop, and an Italian restaurant. It's this amazing ethnic mix that gives Vancouver its flavour. Flavour is used in the literal sense—you can eat in a different ethnic restaurant every week, forever; by the time you eat your way through the yellow pages, new ones have opened up.

"As someone—a writer—remarked while we were

standing in the middle of West Broadway on Greek Day, up to our ankles in discarded beer cups while the loudspeakers pounded out 'Never on Sunday' and small children, large dogs, punks, aging flower children, Point Grey matrons, bikers, students and black-clad Greek grandmothers milled and surged around us, there's as much source material here as anybody could ever want.

"On the other hand, you can walk along Wreck Beach on a weekday in February, or stand under the totem poles in that wild grassy area behind the Museum of Anthropology that overlooks the Point Grey cliffs, and imagine that the last two thousand years have yet to happen."

FIFTY

Dominion Sawmill

RICHARD STREET, NEW WESTMINSTER

The first novelist to describe scenes in Vancouver, Morley Roberts, worked as a labourer during the winter of 1884–85 in New Westminster at the Dominion Sawmill on Richard Street, which is no longer in existence. His 1892 novel, *The Mate of the Vancouver*, qualifies as "the first Vancouver novel." Roberts related his sawmill experiences in his novel, *The Prey of the Strongest* (1906).

Morley Roberts was born in London, England on December 29, 1857. He was educated in Manchester where he began his long friendship with the Victorian novelist George Gissing. After a serious disagreement with his father, who was a tax collector, he set sail for Australia in 1867 and worked in the Australian hinterlands for three years. "I had gone out as a boy and came back a man, for I had had a man's experiences; work, adventure, travel, hunger and thirst." He was a clerk for several years in the War Office and the India Office but left London in 1884 for a job herding sheep in Texas. He took a cattle train to Chicago, worked as a labourer in Iowa and Minnesota, and joined a railway camp in the BC interior. He hiked to the coast in the fall of 1884.

Morley Roberts

In New Westminster, after journeying nearly 8,000 miles in seven months, Roberts had twenty-five cents in his pocket. Extremely well-read and articulate, he took a job as a labourer at the Dominion Sawmill, working from 6 am to 6 pm for thirty dollars a month plus board. Roberts learned some Chinook, completed an autobiography (lost in the mail and never recovered)

75

but was discharged from the mill in March following a fist fight at dinner with a Chinaman. He left for Yale on the Adelaide steamer, worked for a former boss in Kamloops and returned briefly to New Westminster where a second altercation forced a hasty exit. "I thought it best to leave British Columbia, especially as I was told the Chinaman was going to take me to court and I should have been heavily fined if he had." Roberts was to transform these two incidents of uncharacteristic violence into material for fiction.

Roberts left BC via Victoria, worked his way south by doing a variety of unskilled jobs, lived in San Francisco for three months, and returned to London in 1887. He was determined to make his living as a writer. He shared the poverty that George Gissing made famous in his novel *New Grub Street*. He quickly published six novels, six volumes of short stories and two travel memoirs, *The Western Avernus* (1887) and *Land Travel and Sea Faring* (1891). He also impulsively conducted an affair with a married woman, Alice Selous, whom he eventually married in 1893. During the fifteen happy years of his marriage, Roberts wrote twenty more novels (he later dismissed fifteen of these as potboilers), sixteen more volumes of short stories, a volume of essays, *The Wingless Psyche* (1904) and another travel book, *A Tramp's Notebook* (1904).

Illness plagued Roberts and his family. His step-daughter died in 1909 and his wife died of cancer in 1911. "For a year and longer I practically spoke to no one. I was mad if ever man was. I used to go places where they played chess and would play from noon to midnight and never speak a word. Or I wandered about the streets and in and out of cinemas, being all the time in a nightmare." He began to study the nature and causes of cancer. Simultaneously, he published his important fictionalized biography of George Gissing, *The Private Life of Henry Maitland* (1912), his most highly valued novel, *Time and Thomas Waring* (1914), about a man on an operating table coming to terms with physical pain and illness, three more novels, ten more volumes of short stories, three more memoirs, two volumes of verse and another literary study of a friend, *W.H.Hudson, A Portrait* (1924).

In later years Roberts turned increasingly towards his layman's research in pathology and sociology. *Warfare in the Human Body* (1920) and *Malignancy and Evolution: a Biological Enquiry into the Nature and Causes of Cancer* (1926, 1934) essentially theorized that cancer was a response to stress but that tumour formation played a useful evolutionary role in the upkeep of an organism. He turned toward political philosophy with *Bio-Politics* (1938) and *The Behaviour of Nations* (1941). "I never sell," he said. "Oddly enough, if I'm remembered fifty years hence it will be perhaps in the history of cancer research." Morley Roberts died in London on June 8, 1942.

Morley Roberts' novel, *The Mate of the Vancouver* (1892) is a romance initially set aboard a ship called the Vancouver. Thomas Ticehurst, a semi-reluctant sailor, sails from England in 1881 to accompany his brother to the West Coast of North America. He falls in love with a passenger named Elsie, is rejected by her and is stabbed in San Francisco by a villain named Matthias. Matthias goes to jail but vows revenge. Ticehurst recovers and follows Elsie to Victoria. Matthias, who has since killed Ticehurst's brother, finds Ticehurst but loses a final fight with him. Ticehurst finally marries Elsie in Thompson Forks.

Roberts' novel *The Prey of the Strongest* (1906) is a much less melodramatic, more authentic account of working class sawmill life in 19th century BC as Roberts experienced it.

Roberts' made a return visit to "this magic city of El Dorado" in 1926 and was keenly disappointed. "I laughed with sheer incredulity. It could not be! It was impossible and an absurd dream. I found Vancouver something like a Joke of the Gods...I recognized nothing that I knew...A preference for the Renaissance and a passion for thirteenth century ruins cannot predispose the mind to receive kindly the achievements of steel and stone in American-born towers of commercial Babel...The Canadians are not yet wholly Canadians. Sometimes they view the world through spectacles of which one glass is English and one American...Wake up, you dreamer and unnatural Kanuck, and reflect that as a nothern nation you may some day annex the United States!...I own I have never met any Canadian with this notion of the future of his country...To me it seems so historically simple and so natural that I was surprised when some laughed...Here is the possibility of a great city."

FIFTY-ONE

Riverview

HOSPITAL, 500 LOUGHEED HIGHWAY, PORT COQUITLAM

This asylum for the insane is depicted as the Mind Ease Asylum in Julia Henshaw's sophisticated romantic comedy/thriller, *Why Not, Sweetheart* (1901), a novel set in Vancouver and the BC interior.

Julia Wilmotte Henshaw was born in Durham,

England in 1869. She was educated in England, France and Germany and arrived in Vancouver in 1887. Under the pseudonym of Julian Durham she published her first novel, *Hypnotized; or the Experiment of Sir Hugh Galbraith* (1898) and *British Columbia Up-to-Date*. She was editor of the *Province*, Sunday editor of the *Vancouver News-Advertiser* and later an editorial columnist for the *Vancouver Sun*. Her second novel, *Why Not, Sweetheart?*, opens with Jack Maclyn, an independent sportsman, visiting Dr. Dufft at his Mind Ease Asylum overlooking the Fraser River at "the western edge of Canadian soil." Dufft mentions an hereditarily insane Englishman, Christopher Sabel, "a bodily tower and a mental ruin," incarcerated under his care. Maclyn then meets Agnes Arbuckle, a progressive bachelor girl and caustic journalist, and falls in love with Agnes' roommate, the reluctant Naomi. Naomi's guardian, Professor Cyr, discourages Maclyn by declaring himself to be Naomi's fiance. Sabel the madman and the evil professor struggle and drown in a river in the interior. Naomi is free to explain to Maclyn that at seventeen in England she went to the altar with Sabel who went insane during the ceremony, leaving her half-married to him. All's well that ends well when Maclyn marries Naomi and the caustic Agnes also marries the politician Joseph Kingsearl. What the novel lacks in credibility it makes up for in wit.

Henshaw lived on Robson Street and took a keen interest in alpine flora, publishing *Mountain Wildflowers of Canada* (1906), *Mountain Wildflowers of America* (1906) and *Wild Flowers of North American Mountains* (1915). She contributed numerous articles to English magazines, received many decorations for service to the War Effort and was active in Vancouver's high society. She was honourary secretary of the first chapter of the IODE (the Coronation Chapter) for thirty years after its inaugural meeting of August, 1902. In 1914, with her investment broker husband Charles Grant Henshaw, she drove the first motor car across the two divides of the Rockies. Previously her adventurous spirit led her to hike to the sources of the Columbia and Kootenay Rivers in 1896 and to map the interior of Vancouver Island in 1910 and 1911. As an ambulance driver on the Western Front, she received the Croix de Guerre. In the 1930s she moved to Caulfeild in West Vancouver. She died on November 18, 1937.

Riverview's varied associations with Vancouver literature also include Bill T. O'Brien's only novel, *Summer of the Black Sun* (1969), a brave and often remarkable book that is little known despite jacket endorsements from Margaret Laurence, Alice Munro, Eric Nicol, Alden Nowlan and Joyce Carol Oates. While incarcerated in the "Green Lawn" mental institution, protagonist Billy Louper narrates an unglamourous and objective memoir of his past life as a high school athlete and medical student interspersed with anecdotes and reflections from his present life as a "mental patient." "Every character in the world must have been insane at one time or another. I have met the most interesting people here. People who come straight from Charles Dickens and Edgar Allan Poe. They are Dickens and Poe. The only difference is these men are alive, they hurt, they pray, and they cry. I know they cry."

Bill T. O'Brien was born in Princeton, BC in July of 1943. The son of a miner, he attended Tsolum elementary school on Vancouver Island, John Oliver high school in Vancouver, and Como Lake high school. In 1960 he went to Everett Junior College in Washington on a football scholarship. He also briefly played defensive end for the UBC Thunderbirds. His varied work experiences include stints as a logger, guard at Haney Correctional Institute, freelance writer and BC Hydro welder. He now lives and works in Vancouver as a real estate agent.

BC writers Anne Cameron and bill bissett both worked at Riverview. Also see **Sheila Watson** entry (#38).

FIFTY-TWO

Popkum

ON THE TRANS-CANADA HIGHWAY

Delwin Mark Clark

Stranded several nights in a secluded valley near Mt. Thurston, above the unincorporated town of Popkum, a recreational bear hunter narrates D.M. Clark's first novel, *Inside Shadows* (1973), an alarmingly honest descent into the darker recesses of one man's existence. "While I'm up here dying, they're dying down there. Of inertia. Of overindulgence. Of compromise. Sipping drinks, eating peanuts, cramming in chips. Dancing to teenage records, trying desperately to hold on to what little remains of their lives. Pretending to be swingers, wanting to forget yesterday, tomorrow. If the future holds any promise, it's next weekend, the next party. On Sunday mornings they'll rise, hungover, open living room drapes and scream at the kids to turn the goddamn TV down."

The narrator broods about death, imagines insects invading his father's coffin, recalls his painful rejection of the family farm, his overbearing mother, his failed first marriage, his distrust of his second wife's fidelity, his impatience with his children, his humiliating job in his mother-in-law's jewelry store, his useless lust for a junior clerk, his embezzlements and his anti-social self-loathing. "Between my legs the ugliest thing of all—a white, wrinkled worm that spent most of its time in moisture and darkness." Disoriented, weak, and numb, he perseveres, stumbles onto an old logging road, finds the familiar Chilliwack River and doggedly rejoins the world.

Delwin Mark Clark was born in St. John's, Newfoundland on November 20, 1937. He has lived in Chilliwack for most of his life, since age six. Not unlike his fictional protagonist in his two other excellent novels, *The Sunshine Man* (1977) and *Wild Rose* (1982), he spent six months in a fundamentalist gospel school before he was expelled. He worked at a variety of industrial jobs and worked for twelve years as an insurance investigator before turning to writing. Although all three of Clark's novels are published by Canada's largest publishing house, McClelland and Stewart of Toronto, Clark's writing remains one of BC's best kept literary secrets.

"I lived in Vancouver and attended Art School there for a while. I worked there for many years. But I moved back to Chilliwack about twelve years ago because I wanted a quiet place to live and work as a writer. I'm still attracted to Vancouver, and sometimes I miss the desperateness of the city. But for myself and my writing, it's better I stay where I am. I don't have much to do with other writers or artists of any kind, not necessarily because there's anything wrong with that, but because I like it better that way. I'm not much of a 'joiner' and gathering together to bitch and complain, or just talk about writing, is not writing. This area and its surroundings are important to me because of having lived here so long, and the memories that evokes.

"An interviewer once asked me why I used Tsawwassen as a setting for *The Sunshine Man*. She said she couldn't relate to anyone living in Tsawwassen. I asked her why not? Wasn't living and life just as valid in Tsawwassen as in New York, or Paris, or London? That kind of thinking is fading now, I think, and we realize that things happen the same in international places as they do in Vancouver, or Chilliwack, or even Popkum."

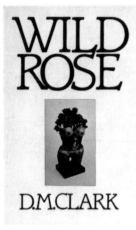

WILD ROSE

D.M.CLARK

FIFTY-TWO

SFU

SIMON FRASER UNIVERSITY

The English Department of SFU has been the second home for the caustic sophistication of novelist John Mills since 1965. This university locale is perhaps fittingly removed and above Vancouver, a city which the English satirist pummelled effectively in his first novel, *The Land of Is* (1972).

"Most of the girls in Vancouver had been a dull lot...girls who wanted you to 'take them out' before they expected you to disarrange their clothing, which meant an hour at some expensive restaurant being bored by the girl's conversation, two hours at a theatre watching some boring play and another hour at what in Vancouver passes for a night club, which means being cramped in a large room shaped and furnished like an army mess hall and being sold costly, diluted drinks and being entertained by talentless dullards from the bottom of some American theatrical agent's list..."

Much of the novel, about twin brothers named Anthrax and Prospero Teitlebaum, is simply a forum for Mills to brandish his wit and hopefully elevate Vancouver from its "Victorian doldrums." As a takeoff on *The Tempest* transplanted to the colonies, *The Land of Is* contains the following footnote: "British Columbia is inhabited by people of many racial origins...though all of them subscribe to the prevailing theory that the province's character should be dominated by the Scottish subculture. Up country the land is owned by American absentee millionaires and farmed by sturdy, lacklustre Neanderthals who vote for Social Credit and profess the heresy of fundamentalism. The poor land is reserved for a variety of Indians—a nation that has been systematically debauched by missionaries, educators, whisky salesmen, politicians and gerrymandering real-estate crooks."

John Mills was born in London, England on June 23, 1930. He came to Canada in 1953 and first travelled to Vancouver, by Greyhound bus, in 1957. He drove west from Montreal with his wife in 1961 and has primarily remained in Vancouver, taking a BA from UBC in 1964 and an MA from Stanford a year later.

"Vancouver was in the early sixties a sleepy and puritanical place fighting for its life, under the leadership of Mayor Tom Campbell, to preserve a nineteenth century atmosphere. Prairie farmers used to come out here to die and be left alone to do so.

Campbell tried to protect them. Thus Vancouver was an interesting place in terms of a revolution taking place in styles, shopping habits, drinking habits, entertainment, etc...I was one of the founding fathers of *The Georgia Straight* and was involved in many of the hassles. These are unthinkable now. So the town was a good place for a writer of satire. I've felt very nourished here. It's a good atmosphere for me to work.''

Mills' second novel, *The October Men* (1973), examines the 1970 FLQ crisis and imposition of the War Measures Act. His third, *Skevington's Daughter* (1978), superbly recalls the decline of counter-culture values and behaviour in Vancouver and West Vancouver. A potpourri of criticism and personal articles, *Lizard in the Grass*, appeared in 1980.

Mills does not consider satire in literature to be a standard Canadian mode. He is thankful for support from Earle Birney and George Woodcock, who have recognized his unique style and high personal standards. "It ought to be remembered that I am not a Canadian writer, though I am a writer who lives in Canada. By this I mean that my themes, style, and view of the world does not conform to CanLit patterns."

FIFTY-FOUR

PACIFIC NATIONAL EXHIBITION GROUNDS

Here Japanese-Canadian citizens were gathered and housed by provincial authorities prior to internment in BC's interior towns during World War II. The wholesale confiscation of Japanese-Canadian properties and suspension of civil rights for 21,000 Japanese-Canadians in BC has concerned numerous writers, most notably Joy Kogawa, whose novel, *Obasan* (1981), is a memoir based on personal experiences and documents of the 1940s.

Joy Kogawa was born Joy Nozonie Nokayama in Vancouver, BC on June 6, 1935. She was the daughter of an Anglican minister. At age six she was shipped with her family to a "shack made of newspaper walls" in the Slocan region of BC. Next the family was transferred to a one room shack in Coaldale, Alberta where her father laboured on sugar beet farms. They then moved to Saskatchewan and Ontario. Kogawa, now divorced with two children, lives in Toronto. She published four books of poetry, *The Splintered Moon* (1967), *A Choice of Dreams* (1974) *Jericho Road* (1978) and *Woman in the Woods* (1985). *Obasan* is a

Joy Kogawa

recollective appreciation of the narrator's aunt "Oba-san" whose resolute endurance in the aftermath of Pearl Harbour's repercussions protected the narrator as a little girl in the Slocan. *Obasan* has been honoured with the Books in Canada First Novel Award, Canadian Authors Fiction Award, Periodical Distributors Paperback Award and literary awards in the US.

The first Canadian writer to present the tragedies and dilemmas of the Japanese-Canadian evacuation en masse was Hubert Evans, whose serialized drama, *No More Islands*, appeared in *Classmate* in 1942 and again in the American church periodical, *Young People's Weekly* in 1943. Dorothy Livesay later wrote a radio play, "Call My People Home" (1950). Japanese-Canadian Ken Adachi (book columnist for the *Toronto Star*) wrote a non-fiction study, *The Enemy That Never Was* (1976) and oral historian Barry Broadfoot published *Years of Sorrow, Years of Shame* in 1977. Roy Miki has edited letters of a Japanese-Canadian journalist to her brother during the evacuation period, *Letters to Wes and Other Writings* (Talonbooks, 1985) by Muriel Kitagawa. Other books on this subject include Jessie L. Beattie's novel, *Strength for the Bridge* (1966) and Shizuye Takashima's children's book, *A Child in Prison Camp* (1971).

One of the shortest and most interesting publications is *What About the Japanese Canadians*, a courageous pamphlet written by Rev. Howard Norman of the St. George United Church in Vancouver for the Consultative Council. Published by the United Church Publishing in 1945, the 32-page, 10 cent booklet credited the role of Japanese-Canadian soldiers in the allied forces and clearly identified the relocation program as racist hatred. "As I write these words," Norman wrote, "Germany is almost out of the fight but Hitler has won a victory in Canada. We have succumbed to his invidious doctrine of racism. When he had finished with the Jews, it was easy for him to proceed with the destruction of other groups within Germany on the grounds that they were a menace to the Reich, the Folk, the Fuhrer. In Canada, under the strain of war hysteria, we have singled out for persecution one of our smaller minorities, seventy-five per cent of whom are Canadian citizens, sixty-one per cent born in Canada—all innocent, on the declared word of our highest authorities, of any crime against Canada."

Another writer who dealt with this issue is Anna Scantland, who self-published *Resignation* (1977) under the publishing name of Parallel Publishers Ltd. **Anna Scantland** was born in 1931 at registered birthplace Sec 2, Tp. 9 W. 3rd, Saskatchewan. Her family moved to Kelowna in 1943. She obtained her BA from UBC in 1955 and married Erik Philip Lund. In 1957, while working at the Hastings Community Centre, she encountered the problems of minority and immigrant people who registered for the English and Newcomers Program. She then obtained her teacher's certificate from the University of Victoria, taught and researched her only novel, *Resignation* (*Shikataganai*) at various universities in the Pacific Northwest. Although the novel intelligently documents the resettlement of Japanese-Canadians in 1941, it is unique in the literature of the internment for clearly emphasizing to the rest of North America's population that it is potentially not immune to abuse of civil rights by government officials. *Resignation* is grounded upon a strong knowledge and understanding of both Canadian and American laws concerning civil liberties.

FIFTY-FIVE

1222

KEEFER STREET

E.G. Perrault's biographical novel about BC timber baron Gordon Gibson Sr., *The Kingdom Carver* (1968), transcribes the address of the Gibson family's first home to nearby Water Street, but the model for the house was located at this address, before the city altered the street plan of the neighbourhood.

E.G. (Ernie) Perrault was born in Penticton, BC on February 9, 1922. His family moved to Vancouver in 1924 and he has lived here since. He attended John Oliver High School and was later influenced by Earle Birney at UBC to become a writer. His brother is Senator Ray Perrault, for many years the major BC presence in the federal Liberal Party. (Gordon Gibson Jr. was an aide to Prime Minister Pierre Trudeau and became the short-lived head of the BC Liberal Party.)

Based on the early years of Gordon Gibson Sr.'s attempts to establish independent logging operation on the west coast, *The Kingdom Carver* is the story of a character named Dave Laird who helps his father log the wilderness area near Klahosat in Clayoquot Sound. Laird meets the proverbial good girl, Sylvia, a missionary's daughter, and the proverbial bad girl, the fiery Teresa. The novel climaxes when Laird frequents a whorehouse on East Hastings called the Palace Royale to celebrate a new sawmill contract. He meets Teresa, learns his contract is a swindle, and flees "the poisoned air" to a major bank where he secures a firm deal to start a cannery. Business success and romantic success with the good girl are sure to follow. The novel cannot

be read as an exact version of Gordon Gibson's beginnings, described in his own bestselling autobiography, *Bull of the Woods* (1980), but there are historical similarities.

Perrault's second novel, *The Twelfth Mile* (1972) is a suspense tale about a towboat operator, Christy Wetholme, who undertakes a routine assignment to bring an offshore drilling rig back to Vancouver. The rig has disappeared, an unidentified Russian ship requires help, and soon Westholme's *Haida Noble* is defying the Canadian Navy and a US battleship at the risk of creating a major military encounter. The adventure-espionage novel is most noteworthy for his admirably accurate portrayal of coastal tugboating as Perrault describes the mechanical and navigational operations of the *Haida Noble*. (Perrault was subsequently hired to write a non-fiction corporate history of Seaboard, the major BC coast exporting firm, to be published in 1986.)

In addition, Perrault has published short stories, radio and television plays, and a third novel, *Spoil!* (1975), an adventure tale based on his five years in the arctic making documentary films. He sees Vancouver as capable of becoming "one of North America's important cultural and international business cross-roads."

FIFTY-SIX

Talonbooks

201-1019 EAST CORDOVA

Up the worn stairs, past the cartons of books and author posters, lies Talonbooks Ltd., owned by Karl Siegler, David Robinson, Peter Hay and Gordon Fidler. The outgrowth of a modest literary magazine called *Talon*, Talonbooks commenced publishing in 1967 and became the foremost publishing house for Canadian plays (such as George Ryga's *The Ecstasy of Rita Joe*, Michel Tremblay's *Hosanna* and *Les Belles Soeurs*, John Gray's *Billy Bishop Goes to War* and Betty Lambert's *Sqrieux-de-Dieu*). Long operated by founder David Robinson (designer of successful Vancouver cookbooks such as Susan Mendelson's *Mama Never Cooked Like This* and *The Umberto Menghi Cookbook*), Talonbooks is managed in 1986 by Karl Siegler and Mary Schendlinger. Its fiction list features work by Marie-Claire Blais, Ken Mitchell, Howard O'Hagan, Jane Rule, Ryga and Tremblay. The press is also responsible for five titles by Vancouver's Audrey Thomas, whose most recent novel, *Intertidal Life* (1984), published by General Publishing, was shortlisted for the Governor General's Award and won the first Ethel Wilson BC Book Prize for Fiction.

Audrey Thomas

Audrey Thomas was born in Binghamton, New York in 1935 and educated at Smith College, with one year in Scotland. She married in 1958 and immigrated to Canada, moving to Surrey, BC in 1959 as a compromise in that it struck her and her British husband as being both British and North American. She received her MA in English from UBC in 1963 and accompanied her teacher husband to Ghana (1964-66), returning to Vancouver in 1967 to give birth to one of her three daughters. That same year her first collection of short stories, *Ten Green Bottles*, appeared with a lead story based upon her confinement and eventual miscarriage in a Ghanian hospital. This six-month experience is expanded upon in her first novel released by Talonbooks, *Mrs. Blood* (1970), in which two symbiotic women, Mrs. Thing, written in the present tense, and Mrs. Blood, written in the past tense, ultimately meld. Two related novellas called *Munchmeyer* and *Prospero on the Island* (1971) explored the symbiotic relationship between a male and female writer while echoing Shakespeare's *The Tempest* with a "magic isle" setting derived from Thomas' associations with Galiano Island. Thomas and her husband separated in 1972.

The first novel Thomas wrote about her New York girlhood, *Songs My Mother Taught Me* (Talonbooks, 1973), once again employed a stylistic narrative friction, this time between Isobel, a narrator in the first person, and Isobel, a character described in the third person. Another novel of schizophrenic tension and an African miscarriage, *Blown Figures* (1974), was published by Talonbooks. Thomas lived in Greece for one year and released an acclaimed collection of short stories, *Ladies and Escorts* (1977), featuring "Aquarius," a story set in the Vancouver Public Aquarium. The novel *Latakia* (Talonbooks, 1979) is about two combative Canadian writers who travel to Greece on a freighter and spend the winter on Crete, where they find their relationship is doomed. Her particularly brilliant collection of short stories, *Real Mothers* (Talonbooks, 1981), chiefly examines family politics. A compilation volume of earlier short stories, *Two in the Bush and Other Stories* (1981), marked Thomas' departure from Talonbooks.

Thomas' *Intertidal Life* (1984) is another autobiographical novel, set almost entirely on Galiano Island, in which her penetrating skills as a "terrible comedian" unfold a retrospective storyline: Alice Hoyle, a love-wrecked mother of three, resentfully recalls the slow capsizing of her fourteen year marriage to Peter, the doting father who commuted to a job and mistresses on the mainland. Best appreciated as a voyage into uncharted waters, it is assertively feminine fiction, to quote Alice Munro's endorsement, where women are "beyond all the fashionable definitions." Alice Hoyle remains faithful to the tides of the moon yet is amongst the vanguard of her sex, compulsively analytical about language and sex. "Women have been shanghaied and now we are waking up and rubbing our eyes and murmuring, 'Where are we?'...Women have *let* men define them, taken their *names* even, with marriage, just like a conquered or newly settled region, *British* Columbia, *British* Guiana, *New* Orleans, *New* Jersey, *New* France, *New* England. I can really understand all those African nations taking new names with their independence."

While Thomas was in Scotland for a one year Canada/Scotland writer exchange program, she expressed her pleasure at winning the inaugural Ethel Wilson BC Book Prize, citing Wilson's influence on her work. She noted that BC, once primarily known for its poets, was developing a varied crop of mature fiction authors.

Of these, **Bill Schermbrucker**, a Capilano College English instructor born in Kenya in 1938, has also published perceptive fiction set in Africa. Schermbrucker's first collection of short stories, *Chameleon and Other Stories*, which appeared in 1983, was also published by Talonbooks. It's a collection of anecdotal nostalgia that doubles as a fictionalized quest for self-definition. Moving to Canada, Schermbrucker connects the two cultures of Kenya and BC with a keen memory for detail and an introspective frankness, allowing readers to make their own judgments on both Kenyan society and the author's personality. The book's title cites Schermbrucker's chameleon-like adaptability as "a muddle-sighted creature."

FIFTY-SEVEN

Press Gang

PUBLISHERS, 603 POWELL STREET

Ironically, or perhaps appropriately, located across the street from a rowdy strip club operated by the Drake Hotel, this is the headquarters of Vancouver's foremost feminist press, Press Gang Publishers, which in 1981 published Ann Cameron's *Daughters of Copper Woman*, a powerful retelling of a mythic West Coast native history based on the oral traditions of Nootka women.

An uncompromising lesbian feminist, Cameron addressed a gathering of women at Nanaimo's Malaspina College following the book's release and said, "The stories in this book are hundreds, if not thousands of years old and were given to me over a dozen years ago by extremely old women on reserves all over the Island. The question that gets asked most about them is 'Is this history or is this fiction?' Nobody ever stops to ask if the crap they push down your throats in school is fiction or history. History as it is taught in the schools is the conquerors' version of what happened. It gets down the throat of the children that they were conquered. So this fiction is as much history as the Battle of Hastings. I happen to feel it's probably closer to the truth than anything that they taught me in school. It certainly has more to do with me as a person who was born on this island, and certainly has more to do with me as a woman, than anything that the school system ever came up with."

Anne Cameron was born in Nanaimo on August 20, 1938. There, under much duress, she raised a family, was divorced and wrote under the name Cam Hubert. "I also lived for a few years in Queensborough, in New Westminster, and enjoyed that very much; it's a working class mixed ethnic mostly immigrant population (or was), so life was varied and interesting. Then I moved to Cloverdale for several years and that was mainly agreeable, although I don't think I'd want to move back again."

Windigo, a stage adaptation of a documentary poem, developed into the first production of Tillicum Theatre, the first native theatre group in Canada. *Dreamspeaker*, a television script directed for CBC by Claude Jutra, won seven Canadian film awards and a first novel award when published in 1979. As the story of an alienated boy and his companionship with an ageing Indian mystic, *Dreamspeaker* was not exactly set in or even near Vancouver. "I tried not to get too location-specific because what I was writing about wasn't—and still isn't—unique to that city. The film was shot in and around the Lower Mainland, and in a couple of places near Nanaimo, but the descriptions of traffic, etc. in the book could as easily apply to the snarled mess going into and coming out of Nanaimo. The facility I had in mind was something along the lines of what Brannan Lake used to be."

Cameron's other acclaimed filmwriting credits include *Ticket to Heaven*, *A Matter of Choice*, *Homecoming* and *They're Drying up the Streets*. Her second novel, *The Journey*, a feminist western cowgirl odyssey, was published in the US in 1982. The same year the first collection of her poetry, *Earth Witch*, was published by Harbour Publishing. Her stage play, *Rites of Passage*, won the New Play Centre's Women's Playwriting Competition in 1975. Cameron has also spent an unsatisfying year with the Film Department of Simon Fraser University. A children's book, *How Raven Freed the Moon*, and another interpretation of a coastal Indian myth *How the Loon Lost Her Voice*, were published in 1985 by Harbour.

Anne Cameron is an outspoken "outsider" who views the privileged patriarchal system of North America as sick. "Since women have started to read and write we have found that we have inherited a flawed tool. Because all the words have been given meaning by someone else, by men. When you say this is National Brotherhood Week it means something wonderful. If you say it's National Sisterhood Week, the president of the bank will crack up laughing... for thousands of years neither the women or the poor were allowed to read and write. It's only recently that women could read and write. I think we've done an incredible job of catching up. I am, I will admit, somewhat of a chauvinist, but I think if you look at Canadian writing over the last fifteen years, the most important stuff has been done by women."

Transplanted by choice from Nanaimo ("Blood Alley") to Powell River ("River City"), Cameron has a view of Vancouver which will never get her work with Jim Pattison's *Beautiful BC* tourist magazine to describe our postcard paradise. "I'm not too impressed with anything at all about Vancouver. I don't like the idea of going to beaches where human sewage is an accepted part of the landscape. The city seems unplanned, as if they are depending on the wonderful scenery to carry it all off. I find the people are great but then most people on the coast are. But Vancouver itself doesn't seem to have any idea of how to be a 'city,' seems more a collection of small town enclaves. If God passed a law that I wasn't allowed to live in the bush, and had to live in a city, I'd go to Toronto where at least they're trying to learn how to live with their citiness. Mostly we call Vancouver 'the big smoke.' Being raised on Vancouver Island, I was pre-conditioned from birth to distrust the place because people who went 'over the water' were heading off either to jail or the 'bin,' which meant to us kids that the place was full of crooks and loonies. We might not have been all that far wrong.

"My kids live there now and I have friends there (Jim Erickson, Hagan Beggs, Daryl Duke, Eleanor Wachtel) but I guess about the time they started to demolish the Alcazar [Hotel], I started to lose interest. I found the Ambassador [Hotel] to replace the old Alcy, but now there are rumours the Ambassador is going to be ripped down, too; which leaves very little there with any character.

"I mean what do you *mean* when you say 'Vancouver' anyway? Most of what *was* Vancouver has been turned into rubble; seems like every time I go down there another piece of Vancouver is gone and what has replaced it is bland 'Anywheresville' stuff. Buildings that could have been used and cherished became something to be wrecked and what has replaced them could as easily be in TennisShoe or TurkeyKnee or a bad Hollywood B-movie about Middle Amerika. And, of course, it doesn't do anything to improve my impressions of Vancouver to know that the place can't even dispose of its own sewage and garbage; first they wanted to export it to Texada Island, then Harwood Island. Well, we don't want it. Dumping that sewage into the Fraser River seems almost pre-deluvian!

"I have always found it interesting that people who live and work in Vancouver think there is some kind of importance connected to being the largest city in the province, but as soon as you get out of Vancouver and into Burnaby, New West, etc, or on a ferry to the Island or the Sunshine Coast, the degree of importance diminishes rapidly. Vancouver is always so busy convincing itself it's Something, and the rest of the province kind of shrugs it off as some sort of aberration. Maybe Vancouver is, in reality, a yappy little maltese trying to get attention. This book, for example, howcum, in Expo year, a book about Vancouver? If Expo is supposed to be a province-wide lawn party...what's wrong with Ladysmith, Coombs, Kaslo, Nelson...why is *all* 'cultural' stuff presumed to revolve around a place where the beaches have become large open-air privies? I guess I kind of share the feeling that Expo (called 'Ego 86' up here) is a *Vancouver* phenomenon, not a provincial one, and I doubt I'll even bother to go down for it. Probably won't be able to afford to get in the gate anyway."

FIFTY-EIGHT

Dunlevy Avenue

(now CENTENNIAL PIER)

In Robert Watson's novel, *Gordon of the Lost Lagoon* (1924), a waterfront waif named Douglas Gordon must live with his alcoholic foster-father in a shack at the foot of Dunlevy, "one of the numerous streets in the vicinity with high-sounding names and disreputable histories."

Robert Watson was born in Glasgow, Scotland in 1882. He came to Canada in 1908 and worked as an accountant for the Hudson's Bay Company for ten years in Vancouver, six years in Vernon, one year in

Robert Watson

Saskatchewan and four years in Winnipeg. In Manitoba he became editor of The Bay's magazine, *The Beaver*. His first novel, *My Brave and Gallant Gentlemen* (1918), is a romantic tale of a man finding love and paradise on the BC coast. *The Girl of the O.K. Valley* (1919) is a similar romance set in the Okanagan, followed by *Stronger than the Sea* (1920), *The Spoilers of the Valley* (1921) and a collection of "western ballads" and poems, *The Mad Minstrel* (1923).

In *Gordon of the Lost Lagoon* the happy Huck Finn existence of Douglas Gordon is shattered by the death of his foster-mother. The boy sells newspapers on a coastal ship, "The Seagull," and befriends a girl named Sheila Campbell in a coastal town called Cohoe (probably Gibson's Landing). In his early manhood he turns down an opportunity to become "the youngest stevedore on the coast" in favour of establishing himself as an independent Howe Sound beachcomber. He finds a lagoon—the lagoon of the novel's title—on an island in the vicinity of Keats Island and stores his logs there. He fights a rival, discovers his parentage and secures Sheila's love. *Secret Harbour* (1926) and *High Hazard* (1928), the latter being an incredible arctic romance serialized in *Maclean's*, also both begin in Vancouver. His final novel, *When Christmas Came to Fort Garry* (1935), is a romance of early Red River days.

"Giving one's formula for writing makes me feel as the bootlegger must have felt before the Royal Commissioner when he was asked to give his recipe for good Home Brew, but I must say that I never make plots," said Watson in 1928. "I create the characters and then let them work out the plot themselves. Sometimes they run away with it and surprise me, but whatever else happens to them I always try to keep the colour of the hair and the eyes of the heroine the same from the first chapter to the last." Watson took his slim talents, his family and his racist tendencies to Hollywood in 1933 where he is reported to have done quite well for himself.

FIFTY-NINE

Hastings Sawmill

BURRARD INLET, FOOT OF DUNLEVY

The first British Columbia novelist to gain popularity within Canada, Frederick Niven, worked at this sawmill in the spring of 1900.

Frederick John Niven was born to Scottish parents in

Frederick Niven

Frederick Niven

Valparaiso, Chile on March 31,1878. He was taken to Glasgow at age five. He worked briefly in his father's cloth business, then as a librarian in Glasgow and Edinburgh. In the early spring of 1899 he arrived in the Kootenay Valley of BC to treat a lung ailment, leaving New Denver for the boomtown of Nelson before coming to Vancouver. In May of 1900 he trekked with two companions the length of the Okanagan Valley and around the Kootenays. Returning to Scotland before Christmas, he began publishing travel accounts in Glasgow, London and in American newspapers and magazines. His first novel, *The Lost Cabin Mine* (1908), was an adventure tale of the Canadian west. He quit journalism to complete his second novel, *The Island Providence* (1910). He married Mary Pauline Thorne-Quelch in 1911. He returned to western Canada on roving commissions as a freelance writer in 1912 and 1913. Rejected for military service, he wrote for the British Ministry of Information during World War I. After three more novels, *Hands Up!* (1913), *Cinderella of Skookum Creek* (1916) and *Penny Scot's Treasure* (1919), he was threatened with a serious heart ailment and moved permanently to BC, at Willow Point six miles outside of Nelson, in 1920.

Niven wrote eighteen more novels in BC. Two historical novels, *The Flying Years* (1935) and *Mine Inheritance* (1940), survey the changes that took place between 1811 and World War I on the prairies. Critic Charles Lillard has described Niven's fictionalized memoir, *Wild Honey* (1927, published in Britain as *Queer Fellows*), as one of the three best early novels of BC in the company of Hubert Evans' *Mist on the River* and Howard O'Hagan's *Tay John*. In his final novel, *The Transplanted!* (1944), Niven dramatizes the economic developments of BC's interior ranching and mining industries and their effects on a broad range of characters. Robert Wallace, a shrewd but visionary Scotsman, becomes a builder of Canada, but others, such as Marion Masters, fall victim of expansionism. The story contains some scenes set in Vancouver.

Prior to his death in 1944 of a heart attack, Niven had become a leading man of letters in Canada and one of the first British writers to effectively establish the first generation of "non-colonial" authors. It was Niven's reader's report to a publisher on Hubert Evans' 1927 novel, *The New Front Line*, declaring "this is a novel that will not go a-begging," that prompted the book's appearance.

SIXTY

312

312 MAIN STREET

The most narratively subtle and thematically complicated novel by a native Vancouverite, Keith Harrison's *Dead Ends* (1981), is primarily a novella-within-a-novel, being written by a Jewish Montrealer named Jessica about an American businessman named Danforth who comes to Vancouver, uses the pseudonym of Eugene Black to investigate Dominion Lumber for take-over purposes, stays at the Bayshore ("like Howard Hughes. And the Beatles."), seduces a Japanese-Canadian dermatologist and is summoned twice to the Vancouver Public Safety Building to identify the corpse of an Italian-Canadian lumber worker from Fraser Street...

If you can follow *that*, you've only begun to unravel the intricacies of *Dead Ends*. *Maclean's* reviewer Douglas Hill has rightly surmised, "Harrison maintains a level of insight and tension...that's consistently high, demanding, rewarding."

Keith Harrison was born in Vancouver in 1945. He left to attend a Ph.D program at Berkeley in 1967, completed his MA, then went to study and teach in Montreal, where he now lives.

DEAD
ENDS

a novel

by

Keith
Harrison

His first novel, *Dead Ends*, was published by Vancouver native and Montreal professor Gary Geddes, who began a unique subscription publishing house from Concordia University, Quadrant Editions. Written in a radically obtuse, introverted shorthand, *Dead Ends* forces the reader to slow down to make sense of the style and content. The novelist within the novel, Jessica, is a speech therapist, would-be author and mother who feels burdened by "the mess of other lives, the ones I'm paid to recreate those I long to create and the one I've procreated." Her work, and Harrison's, is astringently modern. "Nobody describes physical actions in novels anymore; a fight in the sawmill would be vivid, effortlessly, on film. Writers are left wearing tight pants, the shrunken material worn by philosophers after science bleached metaphysics, laundering out physics, the world."

Dead Ends chiefly follows the secretive Vancouver dealings of Danforth, the interloper, who "can't figure out the boundaries of his problems." It's a novel about seeing double: American/Canadian, male/female, fiction/reality, East/West. The scenes in the British Properties, at Wreck Beach, Gastown, Granville Mall (Danforth and Yuki the dermatologist see *Annie Hall* at the Capitol Six) and on Fraser Street are so minutely reproduced and described that *Dead Ends* is almost a strictly Vancouver novel.

The fault of the novel lies chiefly in the complete similarity of style between Harrison's description of Jessica writing her novella, and Jessica's novella itself. The haphazard storyline involving criminality also fails to adequately justify Danforth's ultimate suicide leap from the Lions Gate Bridge. But it's an undeniably strong fictional debut, a book that can best be appreciated by other fiction writers.

A second and slimmer work, *After Six Days* (1985) is a long, fragmented short story about two couples in Montreal in the 1980s. Again Harrison's style is relentlessly sophisticated and he displays an unusual ability to simulate female viewpoints.

As an academic he has written extensively on Malcolm Lowry, and credits the influence of *Under the Volcano* for his division of *After Six Days* between the narratives and lives of four characters. He says being a critic and an academic has been beneficial because those activities have alerted him to "the multiple possibilities of language at any given moment." His prose is riddled with multiple meanings and levels, condensed into as few words as possible. As a teacher he prefers to investigate poetry "for the possibilities of clarity and condensation." If he indeed writes in a distinctively Vancouver-ish style, similar to that of Keath Fraser, Harrison describes that West Coast prose approach as "imagistic, but with rough edges to it." His work in progress is a novel set in France during the French Revolution.

Keith Harrison

Vancouver Police Museum

(formerly CITY ANALYST LABORATORY, MORGUE), 238 E. CORDOVA

The site of the city's pathology lab features prominently in Howard Robens' and Jack Wassermann's co-authored thriller *Hambro's Itch*.

In *Hambro's Itch*, a beautiful concert cellist named Violet Beauman is discovered naked and dead in an $11-a-night Main Street hotel. The authorities cannot determine ʼthe cause of death. The musician has inexplicably slept with a sailor and missed her plane connection. Her lover, an experienced journalist named Martin Albarez, arrives in Vancouver to unravel the mystery. He eventually learns that Violet's estranged father, an American colonel with Pentagon ties, had volunteered his daughter to transport and transmit a deadly virus called Sulfaminophage M 6—"Hambro's Itch"—to Third World countries. The bacteria is designed to destroy only "...the protein poor. The ones with the least intelligence, the ones who've already got everything stacked against them. And, as a group, they're the ones with the highest birth rate." If the world population continues to rise, Pentagon strategists are convinced, one of the twenty countries with nuclear weapons technology is sure to begin a global nuclear war.

Violet was asked by her father to infect the world's poor and weak for humanitarian reasons. She refused, was infected nonetheless, sensed her illness and purposely missed her flight to China by hiding overnight in Vancouver. Albarez pieces together the puzzle and is satisfied the military's fascist elitism has been stymied. But on the book's final pages, a sailor arrives in Hong Kong, seeking a prostitute, remembering a bizarre tryst with a beautiful woman in Vancouver...The plot is intriguing but the jumbled narrative from different time zones, plus the overwritten and cheaply sensationalist prose, makes *Hambro's Itch* a novel that falls far short of its obvious potential.

Howard Robens was born in Mulhausen, Germany on January 2, 1931. He co-authored *Hambro's Itch* with West Vancouver freelance writer and editor, Jack Wassermann. The two men met when their wives shared an office at a New York college. They discovered parallel pasts: both born in Germany, both raised in Israel (at the time, Palestine), both emigrants. Robens visited Vancouver for the first time in 1967 to collaborate with Wassermann on a science text. Robens has since taught at Simon Fraser University, York House, Carnarvon elementary and Eric Hamber high schools. Presently he teaches at Churchill high school. "Vancouver has it all," he says. "I hope we don't waste it. I have lived in many places and none are more beautiful or more temperate in both weather and people. It's a polite, often caring city. But you would never guess at its diversity when you read its newspapers. The city appears too English, too trusting in authority."

Jack Wassermann was born in Dusseldorf, Germany, on April 18, 1929. He has lived in Vancouver since 1966. He describes Vancouver as "a city of delicate flavours adding up to an overall bland taste...overwhelmed by its setting and the edge of the wilderness crowding in...to me, life here has appeared unstressed and friendly (in a cool sort of way)...some "wasp" bigotry, but less than elsewhere...good music...bits of impressive local colour: the hookers (shame on their tormentors!)...recent wave of immigrants...sailboats...the clash and jangle of the West End."

SIXTY-TWO
East Hastings Street
BETWEEN COLUMBIA AND MAIN

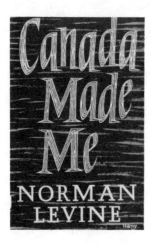

Norman Levine is Canada's most internationally respected male short story writer. He stayed in a seedy, unnamed (and forgotten by Levine) hotel on this block while writing his remarkable travelogue, *Canada Made Me* (1958). A colour photograph of the block adorns Lionel Kearns' poetry collection, *Practicing Up to Be Human*, published in 1978.

"My writing starts with that book," Levine says. His clear views of Canadian mediocrity, complacency, and brutishness were so offensive to our Anglo-Saxon elite when the book was published in England and the US that a Canadian edition of the book was not available until 1979.

Short of funds and preferring the "lower town" areas of cities he visited, Levine fell seriously ill in Vancouver and was generously cared for by an elderly Chinese employee of the hotel. Nevertheless, Levine described his three weeks in Vancouver as the happiest of his entire cross-Canada trip. He made excursions to Victoria and the Cariboo, met literary figures such as George and Inge Woodcock, sailed on a fishboat to Ucluelet and took the ferry across the harbour to North Vancouver for his first visit to an Indian reservation. He was reluctant to leave his tiny Hastings Street room, having discovered a good bookstore (Murray's), the Carnegie Public Library, a late-night cafe that served fresh cod and herring, Harry Harra's fish store on Main, Stanley Park, a nearby Chinese market and a feeling that he could go on writing about his experiences in the city for a long time.

Norman Levine was born in Ottawa in 1923. His father was a pedlar in Ottawa's Lower Town. He joined the RCAF at eighteen, flew the last few months of the war in a Lancaster squadron, attended McGill, edited the university's literary magazine and left Canada in 1949 at the advice of Jack McClelland to pursue a literary career from England. "The English critics had the notion that anyone from the Commonwealth who had the good sense to leave their own country and come to England must be good."

Levine and his family lived a poverty-bound existence, primarily in the coastal town of St. Ives in Cornwall, until his wife's death in 1978. He now lives in Toronto and frequently visits St. Ives. His uniquely subdued and direct stories have been translated into German by Heinrich Boll. His closest literary friends

are Mordecai Richler and Robert Weaver. The latter's
CBC radio program "Anthology" premiered most of
Levine's work.

"I liked it [Vancouver] from the beginning. Gulls and
the sea and things growing. Green, warm, bright light;
no sign of winter. So much for the eyes...One returned
to the shabby stale room, the two calendars, the green
blind, the cracked enamel sink, the iron bed, and felt
happy...

"It was a good place to be alone in. I walked down to
the CPR docks...water. Trees. Mountains. Everything
happened for the eyes. Wherever one walked—no
matter how drab the human in the street—nature
appeared so brilliantly polished. And on other mornings, when it was misty, a fog from the sea, or rain, they
disappeared. Even the streets, the houses, looked
different in the grey light without the handsome
backdrop."

SIXTY-THREE
"The Corner"
HASTINGS AND COLUMBIA

In his Seal Book Award-winning first novel about drug
trafficking in Vancouver, lawyer William Deverell
writes, "In the heart of skid road, yet somehow not a
part of it, there was the Corner, the addicts' Mecca,
their prison, their Emerald City—where the junkies
dance the junkie dance and score the magic powder that
brings their dreams alive, and their nightmares. The
Corner, as a corner, is quite an ordinary intersection,
and tourists might walk by looking for the action and,
not seeing it, shrug and pass on. They might have
found it had they dared enter the dank bistros and beer
parlours nearby, or the greasy coffee salons; and even
then their eyes untrained, they would not have seen the
ritual of the Corner. The rhythms are there to be felt
only by those attuned.

"...The Corner is a community, tight, paranoid,
persecuted like an ancient sect; its membership is
exclusive, the badge of entry being a long narrow tattoo
of scar tissue inside the elbow. There is little trust in this
community, and very little love, but its members,
disgorged from the jails, always return, unable to leave
forever its mystery."

William Deverell was born in Regina, Saskatchewan
in March, 1937. At eighteen, during his first and second
year at the University of Saskatchewan, he took a job as
a police reporter with the Saskatoon *Star-Phoenix.* He

left university for three years to work for the Canadian Press in Montreal and Quebec City, then spent another year at the *Vancouver Sun*. He returned to Regina for his law degree, articled in Vancouver and opened his practice here in 1964. He was elected president of the BC Civil Liberties Association in 1979. He has run unsuccessfully for the NDP in three elections. His first novel was written during a six-month sabbatical at his cabin on Pender Island, where he continues to write his thrillers.

William Deverell is the author of *Needles* (1979), *High Crimes* (1981), *Mecca* (1983) and *The Dance of Shiva* (1984).

SIXTY-FOUR

Columbia Hotel

303 COLUMBIA STREET

The Columbia is mentioned at the outset of Martin Allerdale Grainger's excellent novel of turn-of-the-century logging on the BC coast, *Woodsmen of the West* (1908), as a favourite hangout for loggers in town. The West Hotel, nearby at Hastings and Carrall, also still standing, later became most popular with loggers. Author Rolf Knight has noted miners and railway workers preferred the Cobalt, while a mix of loggers and construction workers generally preferred the Alcazar and the Marble Arch. Other favoured loggers' haunts were the Rainier on Carrall, the Manitoba on Cordova, the Metropole on Abbott and the Rogers on Hastings.

Martin Allerdale Grainger was born in London, England in 1874. He grew up in Australia, won a scholarship to Cambridge, excelled at mathematics, graduated in 1896, set out for the Klondike, was stranded in BC's Cassiar region, worked as a backpacker for the Hudson's Bay Company, reached South Africa after looking after horses for his passage, enlisted in Lord Roberts Horse and returned to BC to do some logging, mining and journalism. He met Mabel Higgs, the sister of his closest friend, on one of the Gulf Islands. Hearing Mabel had left for England, he followed, persuaded her to marry him, and decided to raise money for the marriage by writing a book about West Coast logging. *Woodsmen of the West* (1908), the only book he ever wrote, earned him the equivalent of $300, enough to finance his steerage passage, and his fiancee's first-class passage on the same ship, back to Canada.

Woodsmen of the West is an unusually sophisticated and realistic treatment of rugged "colonial" life for its period. Grainger's autobiographical English narrator observes the "desperate drive-her-under pigheadedness" of a jack-of-all-trades Nova Scotian named Carter who establishes a logging camp at the head of "Coola Inlet." The narrator, as he learns and unfolds Carter's background, is ambivalent about Carter's powerful personality. However, an experienced logger and co-worker, Bill Allen, greatly admires the remarkable Carter, "a black figure of activity." There is minimal plot development, suggesting that *Woodsmen of the West* was directly based on Grainger's own experiences in Knight Inlet.

In 1910 Grainger served as secretary on a Royal Commission to investigate logging practices. He chiefly wrote the Forest Act of 1912, the basis of BC's forest policies and became Chief Forester of BC in 1917. He worked in the private sector, under H.R. Macmillan, from 1920, forming Timberland Investigation and Management Company in 1922, later changed to M.A. Grainger Co. Ltd., headquartered in the Metropolitan Building.

Never a slave to convention, Grainger had his secretary draw an outline of his sole on a piece of paper each year and then dispatched the diagram to an Indian village to have three pairs of moccasins made. (Grainger wore moccasins when he was introduced to King George V in 1920). He died in the offices of well-known Vancouver physician, Dr. Strong, on October 15, 1941.

SIXTY-FIVE

William Hoffer

BOOKSELLER, 58–60 POWELL STREET

W.P. Kinsella

William Hoffer is one of Vancouver's best-known antiquarian booksellers and a dealer in Canadian literature. He has also published numerous broadsides and poetry collections by British Columbia writers in limited editions, and several works of fiction, including George Bowering's *Spencer and Groulx* (1985) and W.P. Kinsella's *The Ballad of the Public Trustee* (1982), *The Thrill of the Grass* (1984) and *Five Stories* (1986).

W.P. Kinsella was born in Edmonton, Alberta on May 25, 1935. He passed his first ten years as an only child in a remote homestead near Darwell, Alberta. Moving back to Edmonton he developed his lifelong fascination for baseball, his other chief fictional subject besides native Indians. In 1967 he opened a pizza parlour in Victoria, having never cooked a pizza in his life. He studied writing at UVic, primarily under W.D. Valgardson. He claims his brief career as a taxi driver in Victoria helped him most to develop his Indian characters. When his first collection of Silas Ermineskin stories, *Dance Me Outside* (1977), appeared, most readers assumed he was Indian. Fans of his later collections, *Scars* (1978), *Gone Indian* (1981) and *The Moccasin Telegraph* (1983) were shocked when Kinsella declared that he didn't care whether or not television and film producers employed real Indians to portray his characters, just so long as they paid him.

Kinsella's first novel, *Shoeless Joe* (1982), a fantastic invention featuring the ghosts of baseball greats and the kidnapping of J.D. Salinger, made Kinsella the first Canadian to win the prestigious Houghton Mifflin Literary Fellowship Award. The author of two other baseball-inspired books of fiction, Kinsella claims to have never played the game in any organized fashion. Each summer he tours the US to attend baseball games. His second baseball novel, is *The Iowa Baseball Confederacy* (1986).

Unusually prolific, outspoken, imaginative and eccentric, Bill Kinsella says he would gladly live in the US except his medical bills would be too high. He lives in a White Rock, BC apartment he purchased with his wife, Ann Knight. Bookseller Bill Hoffer and *Vancouver Magazine*'s Don Stanley, he says, have helped further his career. Kinsella's most recent short story collection, *The Alligator Report* (1985), contains stories mainly set in Vancouver. Kinsella first visited Vancouver on a holiday in 1954 and managed to lose his car at the PNE. Nonetheless, Kinsella says, "Vancouver is the most beautiful large city in Canada, by far. The downtown has not been blasted and rebuilt to nearly the extent, say, Edmonton or Calgary has. The climate is wonderful. It has no disadvantages I can think of except perhaps the 'union mentality' that keeps the economy in chaos."

SIXTY-SIX

Travellers Hotel

57 WEST CORDOVA

The drug trafficking narrator of John Birmingham's novel, *The Vancouver Split* (1973), frequents this hotel

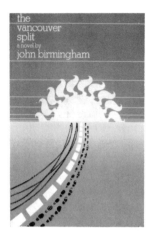

and the nearby Gastown Inn (now the Cambie Hotel) to sell drugs to transients in the early 1970s.

The young American narrator with the self-described "face of an angel and the heart of a devil" recounts his escapades in Vancouver and at Long Beach in retrospect from a New York sanitarium. The novel is remarkable in that surprisingly little readable fiction documents the heydays of hippiedom in Vancouver, and, for a novel published by a twenty-one-year-old, *The Vancouver Split* is unusually free of self-glorification, undue posturing and sentimentality. The vagabond protagonist visits the Children's Aid Society on Broadway, the Catholic Charities Hostel, the Beatty Street Armoury hostel, a Jethro Tull concert at the Agrodome, the Cornwall Street feed-ins, Kool-Aid, the White Lunch cafeteria on Hastings and attends a Laurel & Hardy flick at the Magic Theatre while on acid. Vancouver "was an easy place to live with little money. No jobs were available and everybody seemed to be on welfare. The conservative mayor was trying to change the situation; run the hippies out of town; but in the meantime there were two feed-ins in a schoolyard every day, and the town was loaded with free hostels."

John Birmingham was born in New York City in 1951. At eighteen he mailed his first book, *Our Time is Now: Notes from the High School Underground*, in manuscript to Kurt Vonnegut, who furnished an introduction to it.

Two thinly fictionalized memoir-novels by Victoria resident britt hagarty, *Prisoner of Desire* (1979) and *Sad Paradise* (1981), cover much the same territory but lack craftsmanship and editing. John Lazarus' light comedy of manners, *The Late Blumer*, about a displaced hippie recovering from an LSD trip fifteen years later, enjoyed commercial success in 1984–85. Also see **John Mills** entry (#53).

SIXTY-SEVEN

Victory Square

HASTINGS AND CAMBIE

Earle Birney, Vancouver's most central literary figure for many years, rallied the unemployed to his Trotskyite beliefs here halfway through the city's first 100 years, during the Depression. Consequently, Gordon Saunders, protagonist of Birney's autobiographical depression novel, *Down the Long Table* (1955), fraternizes amongst the under-privileged to learn "when taint rainin', most of us boys'll be settin' in the Sun Parlour—Victory Square to you—it's close and the only park they leave us alone in jis now."

Earle Birney, poet, novelist, editor, professor, dramatist, critic, lecturer and activist, was born in Calgary, Alberta on May 13, 1904. He first came to Vancouver in 1922 to attend UBC, living in an attic at Columbia and 11th Avenue. He worked on the campus newspaper, the *Ubyssey*, and became its editor in 1925, graduated from UBC in 1926, received his Masters from the University of Toronto, studied at Berkeley, taught at the University of Utah in 1930 and studied for his doctoral degree at the University of Toronto in 1933. He became a party organizer for the Trotskyite branch of the Communist Party, taught at Utah one more year, completed his doctoral dissertation on Chaucer in England, worked for the Independent Labour Party and went to Norway to interview Leon Trotsky. He then taught at the University of Toronto and edited the *Canadian Forum* (1938–40) before enlisting for officer training in the Canadian army. His first poetry collection, *David* (1942), won a Governor General's Award. His second collection was *Now is Time* (1945). He edited the *Canadian Poetry Magazine* from 1946 to 1948.

Back in Vancouver, Earle Birney taught medieval literature from 1948 to 1965. At UBC he established Canada's first permanent department of Creative Writing. The list of writers he influenced and encouraged includes many of the authors in this book. His long poem, "November Walk Near False Creek Mouth" (1964) and his verse-play *Trial of a City* (1952) are frequently quoted. His prowess and productivity as an innovative, playful and always evolving poet have shadowed his accomplishments in fiction and non-fiction.

His first novel, *Turvey* (1949), is a comic satire of Thomas Leadbeater Turvey's attempts to join his friend, Mac, overseas by joining the Kootenay Highlanders. Turvey, from Skookum Falls, BC, is made a fireman until he drops a stove lid on his toe and a waiter until he spills coffee down a Colonel's neck. While supposedly guarding the Welland Canal, he is caught AWOL with a girl in Buffalo and held in detention. He is finally shipped to England, where his troubles really begin.

Down the Long Table is the most authoritative fictional account of Canadian leftist activism during the Depression. Only at the close of the novel is the reader aware that *Down the Long Table* is a memoir prompted by its protagonist's appearance before a red-baiting hearing during the McCarthyist purges of the 1950s. Gordon Saunders, a professor of medieval literature at Mormon College in Utah, is "a solitary man stung by the flesh and gnawed by the spirit...a being of grandiose thoughts and microscopic cares, a blocked teacher, a reluctant martyr and a self-betrayed poet." His lover, a well-to-do faculty member's wife, refuses to live with him and subsequently dies of an abortion. Saunders, in Toronto in 1933, pledges to "organize Vancouver" for the Communists, mostly to impress a reluctant fiancee. He rides the freights and rents a $1-a-week flophouse atop the Hotel Universe on Powell Street under the pseudonym of Paul Green.

His migration from effete theorizing to political action organizing the men around Victory Square (from a "universe"-ity job to the real world of the Hotel Universe) reflects the author's own ambivalent attitudes to being "a summer-time rebel." Ultimately Gordon Saunders bids goodbye to Paul Green. He returns to teaching, pronouncing himself still a fool, but no longer an arrogant one. "Goodbye to all the ragged, flea-bitten perpetually defeated legion whose rallying ground was Victory Square," he says, "whose boney arms dipped for the daily butts in the morning gutter and were raised in helpless afternoon defiance before the surly clerks of the relief offices and the virtuous faces of merchant-aldermen—and who were too proud or too doctrinaire to beg dimes from the blue-jowled owners of Buicks and went hungry and alone to their lousy evening beds."

Birney comments, "The characters were from life, that summer of '33, but the melodramatic ending is fiction. The Square was the prole forum, debating society and general bullshit centre."

Earle Birney lives in Toronto.

SIXTY-EIGHT

Vancouver School of Art

DUNSMUIR AND HOMER (original location)

Jim Willer

Prior to the 1980s when "the Art School" became the Emily Carr School of Art on Granville Island, the grey Art School building was a lively cultural hub for artists such as Jim Willer, author of *Paramind*. Willer arrived in Vancouver in 1964 to teach at the Art School at the request of painter Takao Tanabe.

Jim Willer was born in Winnipeg on February 25, 1921. He first saw Vancouver in 1949 while on a bus tour to Los Angeles. "Vancouver obviously had a whole different aura to me," he recalls. "Being anarchic in spirit, I felt comfortable in spirit here immediately. I was also especially attracted to the

Haida art." After graduating from United College in Winnipeg, Willer went on a painting tour of western Canada with Joe Plaskett. With the support of Lawren Harris, he won a Canadian overseas award to study at the Royal Academy of Amsterdam. He lived and studied throughout Europe for two years on $2,000, having developed a Bohemian lifestyle for the sake of art. As well as being an artist, sculptor, mural painter and maker of toys for adults, Willer also maintained an interest in writing.

"Around 1961 we started to hear reports on the radio about computers going berserk, that sort of thing. Of course it was rubbish but it set me thinking that it might be possible for machines to evolve in their own right. I began to ask myself about the possibilities for non-protein intelligence. I was writing *Paramind* in my head from about 1963 on. I talked to everyone about it, bored all my friends to death with it, until one day my wife came home from her job at the Vancouver Art Gallery and told me about this literary competition being sponsored by the Imperial Tobacco Company for Canada's centennial." Willer wrote most of his futuristic entry, *Paramind*, on a farm in Point Roberts.

Paramind is a puzzling, sophisticated, dated and intense experimental novel of the 21st century. It is an anti-Utopian vision of "electric government." "In the library it's filed under science fiction," says Willer, "but I call it my 'holy book.' I hope there's a lot of humanity in it." *Paramind* split the $33,000 prize with two non-fiction manuscripts. With his share Willer began to build his present home at Sunset Beach with the help of sixty-five volunteers. Willer and his wife had previously been living in a log cabin on Copper Cove Road in West Vancouver, where they were frequently visited by Willer's only primarily literary acquaintance, Earle Birney (one of the five judges for the Imperial Tobacco Centennial Award for Canadian Writing).

Raven Steals the Light (1985) by acclaimed Haida artist and carver Bill Reid, with the assistance of book designer and poet Robert Bringhurst, is another example of a prose fiction work by a Vancouverite who is primarily an artist. The interpretive retelling of the well-known Raven legend is illustrated by Reid's drawings.

Nootka artist George Clutesi has also published Indian stories, including *Son of Raven, Son of Deer: Fables of the Tse-shaht People* (1967) and *Potlatch* (1969).

SIXTY-NINE

700 HAMILTON

Norman Newton

Long a bastion of literacy and intelligent commentary on the arts, the CBC Vancouver headquarters has also long employed radio producer Norman Newton, an accomplished novelist, born in Vancouver.

Norman Newton was born in Vancouver in 1929. A former actor who has been active as a radio playwright since the early 1950s, Newton also worked as a tugboat deckhand and as a mess-boy on a freighter between Ireland and Canada. Since joining the BBC in London, his radio and stage plays include *The Death of the Hawk, The Rehearsal, The Abdication* (revised as *The Antiquarian*), *The Lion and the Unicorn* (retitled *The Choice of Hercules*), *King Orpheus* and a translation of Moliere's *The Misanthrope*.

Newton has published two historical novels. *The House of Gods* (1961) is about the Aztecs; *The One True Man* (1963), based on a research trip to Mexico, speculates that the Phoenicians established colonies there. His satire on a fictitious BC lumber port called St. Charles, *The Big Stuffed Hand of Friendship* (1969), exposes the hypocrisy and immorality of BC's treatment of native Indians after a sex-starved Anglican pop-pastor-cum-beatnik named Reverend Grubb forsakes Vancouver to live amongst the villagers. A schoolteacher speculates BC was discovered first by Mexicans. The Dean of Canadian Poetry, a Dr. Garth MacDonald, lectures on the essential quality of Canadian poetry as recorded on the women's page of the *Port Charles Recorder*. Most characters in the book drastically overestimate their own importance. Ultimately the pulp mill community erupts into racial rioting. An authority on Northwest Coast Indian mythology, Newton later published a non-fiction study of the Haida Indians, *Fire in the Raven's Nest* (1973).

Besides Newton, Robert Harlow and Christopher Hyde, another novelist who has worked for the CBC is **Ray Ostergard**. Born at Staines, Middlesex, England on July 26, 1937, he was raised at Stonehouse, Scotland, and upon his mother's re-marriage, "was shipped with my younger brother and a good deal of hope to Canada." He came to BC in 1945, lived in Port Moody and Quesnel before attending UBC for four years, and worked at a variety of jobs in Vancouver that included some work for the CBC. His slim comic novel, *The Vernal Equinox* (1964) celebrates the first day of spring in Vancouver with over-explained narration and mundane dialogue. Whereabouts unknown.

SEVENTY
Alcazar Hotel

CORNER OF DUNSMUIR AND HOMER (demolished 1983)

Peter Trower, author of a forthcoming fiction collection and one of BC's finest poets, published a memorial article on the Alcazar Hotel in the April, 1983 issue of *Vancouver Magazine.* He drank there often in the 1960s with the likes of Al Purdy, John Newlove and Milton Acorn when the Alcazar was a favoured hangout of writers and students from the Vancouver School of Art nearby. In addition, Trower lived in the Alcazar on numerous occasions during the periods when he was a logger.

ALCAZAR REQUIEM

Wind whitecapping the inlet—
rain like whipping string—
Sea-Bus bucking and dipping—
behind us—the Alcazar, dead as a doornail.

Landmark of brick and lumber
soon to be sundered and tumbled
in a rattle of empty rooms
all of the ghosts going down in a heap.

The bar where we tippled and quipped
safe in our roles and phases
is a circus of empty chairs
the clowns are gone with a vanishing giggle.

The jokers we fancied we were
on countless immoderate nights
have followed their antic thirsts
away from this cold and cancelled arena.

Plane shaking down the blow—
raingrey city receding—
yesterday closing its books—
evening Sea-Bus bouncing me home.

—1983, revised 1984
(previously unpublished)

Peter Trower

Peter Trower was born at St. Leonard's-on-Sea, England on August 25, 1930. Following the death of his test pilot father in a plane crash, he and his mother and brother came to Canada on an evacuee ship in 1940. That year they stayed with Trower's aunt on Nelson Street in the West End. Trower quit school to work in logging camps. A film of Trower as the logger-poet, *Between the Sky and the Splinters*, was filmed at Jackson Bay.

For twenty-two years, when Trower wasn't haunted by the physical hazards of the logging industry, he haunted various scruffy rooming houses and hotels such as the Alcazar, the Cecil and the Marble Arch. He now lives primarily in Gibsons, turning increasingly to prose to make a living. A collection of his semi-fiction, *The Camp Drifters*, is slated for publication in 1986.

"When I first saw Vancouver in the summer of 1940, it was a pretty unsophisticated place—basically a milltown that had burgeoned into a city of much rough-hewn charisma but little culture. Horse-drawn bread and milk wagons still trundled along the streets of a West End innocent of high-rises, where home owners still burned sawdust in the basement furnaces of big frame houses....Today the downtown core is totally altered and the city has acquired a certain veneer of sophistication. But underneath it all, Vancouver's small town roots still show through. I hope they always will."

The bar of the Cecil Hotel on Granville arguably eclipsed the popularity of the Alcazar as a watering hole for writers in the early 1970s when UBC produced a bumper crop of aspiring writers in the city. At the time, the Cecil was the closest downtown bar to the university. But the convivial atmosphere there, too, has been demolished—not by the wrecking ball, but by the trend to turn disrespectable beer parlours into respectable strip joints in the 1980s.

SEVENTY-ONE
Literary Storefront
314 WEST CORDOVA

The Literary Storefront, upstairs at this address, was a rare common ground for Vancouver's writers from 1978 until a lack of operating funds forced its closure in 1984. It was opened by poet Mona Fertig and was ostensibly modelled on Sylvia Beach's famous bookstore and writers' meeting place in Paris, although the Storefront never actually functioned as a bookstore. Among the many literary friendships formed thanks largely to the Storefront is the unique professional relationship between novelists Blanche Howard and Carol Shields.

Blanche Howard was born in Daysland, Alberta on November 7, 1923. She first came to Vancouver in 1939 when her father took the family to the coast to see the newly completed Lions Gate Bridge. She graduated in science from the University of Alberta, worked as a chartered accountant, then took up writing when her husband was elected to Parliament in 1968. Her first novel, *The Manipulators* (1973), won the Canadian Booksellers Award. *Pretty Lady* (1976), a second novel, is set largely in North Vancouver where Howard now lives. Examining the past of a vain and domineering mother nicknamed "Pretty Lady," a son and daughter discover she once gave birth to a stillborn, bisexual, deformed child after having sex with her twin brother during an Iowa hurricane. The sensational Gothic culmination is strangely at odds with the sober and intelligent development of the novel. Howard's third novel, *The Immortal Soul of Edwin Carlysle* (1977), employs the author's training as a physicist to reveal "the perilous border between genius and madness" in its protagonist, Edwin Carlysle, who uses science to "unlock the secret of man's immortal soul." Carlysle's wife is intolerant of his double nature and is drawn to Carlysle's best friend, but Carlysle finds another woman to understand and support his mental adventuring.

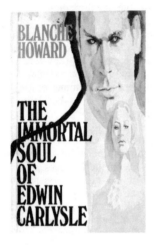

Carol Shields was born in Oak Park, Illinois on June 2, 1935. She taught at UBC in 1979-80. Only the first thirty-four pages of her second novel, *The Box Garden* (1977), are set in Vancouver. Her other novels, which are low-key explorations of contemporary female dilemmas, are *Small Ceremonies* (1976) which won a Canadian Authors Association Award, *Happenstance* (1980) and *A Fairly Conventional Woman* (1982). She is also the author of two books of poetry, a work of criticism and a collection of short stories, *Various Miracles* (1985).

Both Storefront supporters, Shields and Howard decided to continue their friendship when Shields moved to Winnipeg to teach at the University of Manitoba, by co-authoring a novel. The result, *A Celibate Season*, is about a married couple separated by BC's recession. The collaborative story evolved as a novel of letters between a wife working in Ottawa (Shields) and a house-husband in North Vancouver (Howard). Despite Carol Shields' rising reputation as a novelist, *A Celibate Season* has yet to find a publisher due largely to its inclusion of political material specifically germane to BC. "I'm sure if we had the same amount of local Toronto colour," says Howard, "we wouldn't be having the same difficulty getting it into print." Despite the supposed ascension of BC publishing into a multi-million dollar industry, almost all novels written by British Columbians still must seek publication in Ontario or the US.

SEVENTY-TWO
Piccadilly Hotel
620 WEST PENDER

Perhaps the only literary genre indigenous to Canada was born in the bar of the Piccadilly Hotel. Here Steve Osborne, Mary Beth Knechtel, William Hoffer, Laura Lippert and D.M. Fraser devised the Pulp Press Three-Day Novel in 1978.

Steve Osborne, with his brother Tom, was for many years the centre of Pulp Press. Mary Beth Knechtel is an editor who published one book of fiction, *The Goldfish That Exploded* (1978), "a potboiler for disillusioned aesthetes." William Hoffer is one of Vancouver's leading antiquarian booksellers and also publishes broadsheets and literature in limited editions. Laura Lippert was a typesetter at Pulp Press and a writer. For information on **D.M. Fraser** see entry #39 in this book.

The Pulp Press International Three-Day Novel Writing Contest invites contestants to complete a novel over the Labour Day weekend. After the entries have been submitted to sponsoring bookstores, Pulp Press determines finalists and ultimately publishes one winner. The first winner was Tom Walmsley's *Doctor Tin* (1979), probably the most legitimate three-day novel to have been awarded the prize. It is a crazed detective-style rockumentary which tapers into confusion. The other winning books are Ray Serwylo's *Accordion Lessons* (1981), a well-crafted and memorable story about growing up Ukrainian in Winnipeg; bp Nichol's *Still* (1982), an avant-garde dud by a Toronto poet who was born in Vancouver in 1944; Jeff Doran's *This Guest of Summer* (1984), an engaging tale of an urbanite who buys a ramshackle house in rural Nova Scotia only to discover the area is creepy with incest; and Jim Curry's *Nothing So Natural*, a childhood memoir of a disturbed family. The 1985 contest winner is Marc Diamond, an SFU professor whose book, *Momentum*, appeared in 1986. Each year the contest attracts wider publicity and more entrants.

Pulp Press was formed by Steve Osborne in 1971. It has been one of the few Vancouver publishing companies to consistently publish literature. The company has evolved through various forms of co-operative ownership and financial turbulence.

Initially situated at 440 W. Pender Street near the Marble Arch Hotel, Pulp moved to 572 Beatty Street and then to its present premises at 986 Homer Street.

SEVENTY-THREE

Vancouver Post Office

GRANVILLE AND PENDER (former location)

Based upon the volatile aftermath of the 1938 occupation of the post office by unemployed "sit-downers" for nineteen days, Irene Baird's novel *Waste Heritage* (1939) has been touted as the classic novel of the Depression in Canada. "I think it is one of the best books that has come out of Canada in our time," wrote Bruce Hutchison. George Woodcock has also praised the novel. A reviewer for the *Globe and Mail* called *Waste Heritage*, "The only piece of Canadian fiction on this topic which could be compared for quality with *Grapes of Wrath*."

As the most famous expression of labour unrest in Vancouver's history, the post office occupation sparked a protest trek to Victoria in which the characters of *Waste Heritage* participate.

Irene Baird was born in Cumberland, England in 1901. She came to Vancouver with her parents in 1919 and worked as a journalist for the *Sun* and the *Province*. *John* (1937), her first novel, is a character study of philosophical Scot named John Dorey who homesteads on a ten acre Vancouver Island retreat.

Her second novel, *Waste Heritage*, follows the plight of aptly-named Matt Striker, a twenty-three-year-old Saskatchewan resident, and his simple-minded companion Eddy, who is obsessed with one day getting a new pair of shoes. The novel has obvious echoes of Steinbeck's *Of Mice and Men*, which had appeared two years earlier. Naive and reluctant to agitate against authorities, Matt and Eddy endure poverty and confusion, seeking a fair deal after six years of steady job seeking and drifting. Matt is arrested. Eddy dies. Although the novel is dedicated to "Matt and to Eddy and to the other Hundred Thousand," it is evident from the writing that the story was derived mainly from the author's sympathies rather than direct experiences. Most of the dialogue is forced and unnatural. ("Gee," Hazel said, "it must be swell to win a sweep or something") and the place names are unnecessarily fictionalized. Vancouver is "Ascelon" and Victoria is "Gath."

Irene Baird's third novel, *He Rides the Sky* (1942), is

a series of letters from a young RAF pilot to Victoria prior to his death defending London during the Blitz. Her final novel, *Climate of Power* (1971), reveals the federal government's misguided attempts to improve Inuit culture. In 1942 Baird worked for the civil service and became chief of information for the Department of Indian Affairs and Northern Development. She died in 1981.

A mail sorter and mail handler at the current Vancouver Post Office, **Don Austin** was born in St. John's, Newfoundland in 1946. He moved to Vancouver in 1974. His first major book of fiction, *The Portable City* (Pulp Press, 1983) is a collection of twenty-eight short pieces, fantastic and varied creations in themselves which cumulatively are playful exercises that are forgettable. A new collection, *The Lost Tribe* was published by Pulp Press in 1986.

SEVENTY-FOUR

Bank of Montreal

GRANVILLE AND PENDER

The first specific locale mentioned in the fifteen novels of Harold Bindloss which are partially set in Vancouver is the Bank of Montreal. Harry Alton, the rancher hero of *Alton of Somasco* (1906) enters the bank and takes a young lady to breakfast. This earliest "Vancouver novel" by Bindloss contains an enthusiastic description of "a new stone city which had sprung, as by enchantment, from the ashes of a wooden one, and would, purging itself of its raw crudity, rise to beauty and greatness yet." In truth, Bindloss' memories of Vancouver were vague and his references to the city reveal very little.

Harold Bindloss was born in Liverpool in 1866. He spent several years at sea, visiting Africa and Canada, before returning to London in 1896 and entering journalism. Poor health persuaded him to compose novels and stories of romantic adventure in the colonies, which found a wide audience in England. His first book was non-fiction, *In the Niger Country* (1898), but then Bindloss proceeded to churn forth over sixty novels. Three more Bindloss novels were published posthumously. Very little has been recorded about his private life. He died on December 30, 1945 in Carlisle, England; an obituary article was printed in the New York Times on January 2, 1946. Bindloss, Alberta bears his name.

Most of Bindloss' novel were published in the United States with different titles. Bindloss' Vancouver novels include *Alton of Somasco*, *A Damaged Reputation*, *Delilah of the Snows*, and *A Sower of Wheat*, among others.

Bindloss' many Vancouver-related novels were the first in a long tradition of "go-west-young-Brit-go-west" novels which culminated in a sophisticated but little-known work by a writer named **Magnus Pyke**. Angus Hake, the subject of Magnus Pyke's novel of light cynicism. *Go West, Young Man, Go West* (1930), works primarily as a clerk for the Consolidated Bank of Canada at Tenth and Trimble (a corner at which four banks are presently located).

Hake, an Englishman, first studies farming at McGill for two years: "I had cut myself off from polite young men who allow themselves to be put into family businesses or supported by genteel remittances from their grandparents, and come to a country where education is looked upon with amusement, money with respect and manual labour as something that any man may do." Hake then arrives at Vancouver's CPR "palace" at the outset of the story and, like so many other Englishmen, is unimpressed. "I stood below the monumental cement pillars and took in my first view of Canada's Gateway to the Pacific. Sombre brick houses in front of me, to the left more dismal erections, to the right, the iron railings of a bridge, with water gleaming mysteriously. An engine hooted like a dying elephant..." Disenchanted with his efforts to become a farm labourer ("It seemed impossible that I had ever lived a civilized life in England") he accepts the assistance of a well-established family from England, the Burtons, and begins his half-hearted career as a bank clerk. Hake is swindled but good-naturedly accepts his fate as a sophisticated newcomer in the unsophisticated west. Unlike Bindloss' novels in this genre, *Go West, Young Man, Go West* remains readable and was undoubtedly based on the author's firsthand experiences in Vancouver.

SEVENTY-FIVE

"Pender Hall"

CORNER OF PENDER AND HOMER

The city's most enthusiastic reception for any writer in its history was accorded to Rudyard Kipling when he addressed the Canadian Club at the Acland-Hood Hall, known as Pender Hall, on October 7, 1907, the year he received the Nobel Prize for Literature.

Rudyard Kipling (1865-1936) was the English novelist and poet most renowned for his stirring glorification of the British Empire and English imperial values. Kipling was greatly impressed by Vancouver during his wedding tour of North America in 1892, and was encouraged by the efficiency of the Royal Canadian Mounted Police. "Always the marvel to which Canadians seem insensible," he wrote, "was that on one side of an imaginary line should be Safety, Law, Honour and Obedience, and on the other, frank, brutal decivilization."

Kipling was so pleased with Vancouver and its prospects that he purchased a town lot in the Mt. Pleasant area (subdivision 264A, Ward Five) prior to embarking for Japan from the CPR dock on the Empress of India on April 4, 1892. "He that sold it to me was a delightful English boy," Kipling later wrote in 'American Notes.' "All the boy said was, 'I give you my word it isn't on a cliff or under water, and before long the town ought to move out that way.' And I took it as easily as a man buys a piece of tobacco. I became owner of 400 well-developed pines, thousands of tons of granite scattered in blocks at the roots of the pines, and a sprinkling of earth. That's a town lot in Vancouver. You or your agent hold onto it till property rises, then sell out and buy more land farther out of town and repeat the process. I do not quite see how this sort of thing helps the growth of a town, but the English boy says it is the 'essence of speculation' so it must be all right. But I wish there were fewer pines and rather less granite on the ground."

Kipling was rather less pleased with Vancouver when he returned in 1907. "Such a land is good for the energetic man," he observed. "It is also not so bad for the loafer." He learned that the property for which he had been paying taxes was legitimately owned by someone else. Kipling, the great man, had been swindled. He published newspaper articles praising the enterprising west coast whalers and analyzing British Columbia's racist problems with the influx of Hindoos [sic] but nary a word appeared in public print about his property loss. Privately, Kipling wrote, "All the consolation we got from the smiling people of Vancouver was: 'You bought that from Steve, did you? Ah-hah, Steve! You hadn't ought to ha' bought from Steve. No! Not from Steve!' And thus did the good Steve cure us of speculating in real estate."

When Kipling arrived in Vancouver in 1892, the City Solicitor named St. George Hamersley, a member of the Inner Bar, London, was asked if he might greet the visiting writer named Kipling. "Kipling! Who the devil is Kipling?" the lawyer reportedly said. "Never heard of the man!" Fifteen years later Kipling was met by the

Mayor, presidents of the Board of Trade and the Canadian Club and provincial government members. An overflow audience of over 500 attended his luncheon speech to the one year old Canadian Club at Pender Hall. Women weren't invited; there was not enough room. But women came anyway, crowding the hall to its doors, filling the spectator gallery. "There is a crafty network of organizations of business men called Canadian Clubs," Kipling subsequently wrote. "They catch people who look interesting, assemble their members during the mid-day lunch hour, and, tying the victim to a steak, bid him discourse on anything that he thinks he knows."

After receiving an unprecedented standing, cheering ovation and a moroccan leather case, embossed with his initials, containing his honourary lifetime membership to the Canadian Club, Kipling rose to discourse on Vancouver. He compared the city to the head of an army bravely passing through the mountains "to secure a stable Western civilization facing the Eastern Sea." Frequently interrupted by applause, he added, "If I had not as great faith as I have in our breed, and in our race, I would tremble at your responsibilities." When later asked by a reporter for the *Vancouver World* newspaper about "the all-absorbing topic of Hindoo immigration," Kipling confided he "had come six thousand miles to study it." He added, "I have seen the Hindoos in many places and they are the same all over except that here they seem to be more timid and weak than is their wont." Kipling concluded this was due to the weather.

Another Nobel Prize-winning author, Sir Rabindranath **Tagore** (1861-1941), who received his Nobel Prize six years after Kipling, had a much less pleasant visit to Vancouver. During his fourth visit to North America in 1940, the Hindu poet, mystic and educator was detained by US immigration officials and cross-examined about the purposes of his tour. He telegraphed President Roosevelt from Vancouver about the incident but never received a reply. He cut short his tour and returned to India. Tagore, also known as Ravindranatha Thakura, did not find Commonwealth countries were much more enlightened than the US. Knighted in 1915, he had resigned the honour in 1919 in protest against British repressive measures in his native country.

SEVENTY-SIX

Abbotsford Hotel

921 WEST PENDER

Thomas MacInnes

Here Tom MacInnes lived and wrote his 170-page anti-Oriental treatise, *Oriental Occupation of British Columbia* (1927). "Pender Street is triumphant. Insidiously but surely and with marked acceleration every year, it is establishing glorified extensions of itself along Robson Street, Davie, sections of Granville, and a dozen or more commercial streets of Vancouver upon which, even so short a while as ten years ago, not a single Chinese or Japanese shop was to be found."

Thomas Robert Edward MacInnes was born near Dresden, Ontario in 1867. He moved with his family to New Westminster as a boy. He attended Osgoode Hall in Toronto, participated in the Yukon gold rush, then settled in Vancouver as a lawyer. From 1916 to 1927 he spent long periods in China developing business interests. He was the only foreign director of the Kwontong Tramway Company from 1919 to 1924. When the Chinese revolutionary government expropriated his company, MacInnes became actively racist.

(Dr. Sun Yat Sen, who led the Chinese revolution in the late eighteen and early nineteen hundreds had come to Vancouver three times to live and raise funds, and had lived on West Pender himself, at Pender and Abbott, directly across from the new Sun Yat Sen Hanging Gardens, built in 1985.)

MacInnes published a series of articles in the *Vancouver Province* and the *Vancouver Morning Star* in 1926 which were the basis of *Oriental Occupation of British Columbia*, published by the Sun Publishing Company. MacInnes urged BC to adopt apartheid-like policies favoured by the Dominion of South Africa. He primarily feared that an influx of Oriental merchants would depreciate real estate values. "I'm no fanatic or unsubstantial alarmist," he wrote. "Fifty years hence, if there still be any copy of this book left in British Columbia, I hope some more or less fair Nordic reader will be in a position to smile at the fears expressed in it." Fifty-two years after MacInnes published *Oriental Occupation of British Columbia*, Vancouver journalist Doug Collins published his book *Immigration, the Destruction of English Canada*.

MacInnes was chiefly regarded in his day as a poet for his book *Roundabout Rhymes* (1923). He published an earlier record of his Chinese experiences, *The Teaching of the Old Boy*, and a prose collection about Vancouver called *Chinook Days* (1926).

115

MacInnes was the son of a lieutenant-governor of British Columbia, Thomas McInnes, but he changed the spelling of the family name. As a lawyer he was secretary to the Bering Sea Commission and helped draft immigration laws in 1910. He died in Vancouver in 1951.

The most offensive racist novel published in BC is Hilda Glynn-Ward's *The Writing on the Wall* (1921), also published by the Sun Publishing Company. This propaganda tract concludes with Vancouver's white population dying from typhoid fever contracted from Chinese-grown vegetables and sugar to which the local Chinese merchants had purposely added typhoid germs. The Chinese and Japanese remain healthy and triumph because they have been "inured to it by countless generations of living without sanitation."

In 1921 Japanese and Chinese immigrants comprised one per cent of the Canadian population but seven per cent of BC's population. The vile fears expressed in *The Writing on the Wall* reflect the anglophilic dread of BC's ruling class for the so-called "yellow peril." The subsequent incarceration of Japanese-Canadians during World War II was symptomatic of a long and deeply established prejudice against Orientals in British Columbia that *The Writing on the Wall* makes glaringly obvious.

Hilda Glynn-Ward was a pseudonym for **Hilda G. Howard**. She was born in Wales in 1887, daughter of a classical scholar. She travelled extensively, came to Canada in 1910, turned to freelance writing in 1920, primarily lived in Victoria, published a travel book called *The Glamour of British Columbia* (1926) and continued to express her racist views almost until her death in Victoria in 1966.

by H. Glynn-Ward

SEVENTY-SEVEN

Hotel Vancouver

900 WEST GEORGIA

Vancouver detective fiction is highlighted by the climax of *Kosygin is Coming* (1974), written by former Vancouver newspaperman and public relations consultant, Tom Ardies. Atop the Hotel Vancouver, the novel's cop-hero must shoot down a helicopter loaded with explosives in order to save the life of visiting Soviet premier Alexei Kosygin. The book was made into a movie called *Russian Roulette* in 1975, which starred George Segal and was filmed in Vancouver using the roof of the hotel for its climactic scene. The story

A novel by the author of PANDEMIC

follows the attempts of Corporal Timothy Shaver to salvage his reputation by illegally removing a known crackpot named Rudolph Henke from circulation during Premier Kosygin's eight-day visit to Canada. Shaver tries to deposit Henke in the Riverview Mental Hospital, bungles the job and slowly realizes his suspect is a designated scapegoat for a Russian plot to assassinate Kosygin (because Russian generals believe Kosygin is being too soft in negotiating detente with the West). "It's very difficult to kill Kosygin in Russia," says the novel's Russian villain. "But here? This is the ideal place to have it done. Your security is lax and the chances of being caught are remote."

Tom Ardies was born in 1931 and now lives in the United States. His other novels are *Their Man in the White House* (1971), *This Suitcase is Going to Explode* (1972), *Pandemic* (1973), *In a Lady's Service* (1976) and *Palm Springs* (1978).

The first Vancouver mystery novel is *The Black Robe* (1927) by Guy Morton. Partially set in Vancouver, the novel appeared in England as *King of the World* and is especially significant because it is said to be the subject for the second "talkie" financed and filmed outside Hollywood. It was filmed in Victoria.

The Black Robe was **Guy Eugene Morton**'s fifth novel. He was born in York Township, Ontario in 1884. He worked briefly as a schoolteacher before turning to journalism for the *Toronto Daily Star* and the *Globe and Mail*. He wrote sixteen other detective and mystery novels between 1918 and 1936. He died in 1948.

Mystery writer **Maurice Buxton Dix** wrote over fifteen mystery novels including *A Lady Richly Left* (1951) which is primarily set in Vancouver. Dix was born on July 21, 1889 in Middlesex, England. He worked in the English civil service, came to Canada, worked as a bank clerk and fought for four years in World War I. He came to Vancouver in 1930 and published his first novel in 1933. He was hired to undertake a survey of BC libraries. He lived at 1861 Beach Avenue and in the Gleneagles area of West Vancouver, publishing mainly abroad in Commonwealth countries. His whereabouts and fate are unknown.

Raymond Chandler, generally acknowledged as the finest exponent of "hard-boiled" detective fiction, joined the Canadian Army in England in 1917 and was later discharged from the Royal Airforce on February 20, 1919 in Vancouver.

Raymond Thornton Chandler was born in Chicago on July 23, 1888 and died in 1959. His best known works are his first novel, *The Big Sleep* (1939), *Farewell, My Lovely* (1940) and *The Long Goodbye*

Raymond Chandler

(1954), all of which were made into films.

Chandler's final novel, *Playback* (1958), based upon a screenplay of the same name begun in 1947, was set almost entirely in Vancouver. Published in New York as *Raymond Chandler's Unknown Thriller* (1985), the book opens with a beautiful blonde, Betty Mayfield, crossing the border on a train, having narrowly escaped being imprisoned for a murder she did not commit. In Vancouver she becomes once again the prime suspect in a murder investigation. Betty writes a suicide note in the Hudson Bay Department Store but is dissuaded by Brandon, a debonair millionaire who promises to help her by whisking her over to Victoria in his yacht. The Vancouver Police Department's Detective Killaine cleverly determines the murderer is Brandon, who is planning to kill Betty on his yacht. He rescues Betty with a helicopter.

Raymond Chandler

Raymond Chandler was unusually well paid to write this script and took particular care to revise it. Although it contains excellent sardonic dialogue and also takes care to recognize the cultural differences between Canada and the United States, Chandler had difficulty transcribing the story into a novel because the tale was lacking a cryptic first person narrator such as his most famous private investigator, Philip Marlowe.

SEVENTY-EIGHT

Four Seasons Hotel

791 GEORGIA STREET

The penthouse of the Four Seasons is home to the heroin-dealing villains in Jaron Summers' 1981 paperback thriller, *The Soda Cracker*. Corporal Soda (who is nicknamed Soda Cracker because he once ran his motorcycle over the back of a fleeing purse-snatcher) confronts the drug-dealing brothers, Ace and Ivan, in their penthouse suite in order to track down the killer of his partner, Phil (shot during a Sea Festival parade along Georgia Street). The details about Vancouver are imprecise (a yacht is somehow moored in the shadow of the Four Seasons) because the author has only lived and visited in the city for relatively brief periods of his life. "The book explains what happens when the RCMP becomes corrupt, and how it is capable of handling the problem," says Summers. "It shows that Mounties are human beings...that they can make mistakes." *The Soda Cracker* is Summers' first novel, and the first in a series to be based on the adventures of the same Vancouver cop-hero. "There are very few heroes in

Canadian literature," claims Summers. "It's important for any culture to have folk heroes, to make us feel good about our culture. If Sergeant Preston were alive today, this would be his story."

Jaron Summers was born in Calgary in 1942. He attended UCLA to earn a master's degree in TV and film production. His resume states he will go anywhere, anytime, to pursue his freelance career. A current project he devised is a $15-million movie about the 2.2-million-square-foot West Edmonton Mall, to be called *The Mall*. His credits include episodes of *Columbo*, *The Incredible Hulk*, *Hart to Hart*, *Buck Rogers*, *The Overlanders* (CBC) and *CHIPS*. His *Hart to Hart* episode was about a woman who disposed of her husband by spraying him with a perfume which enraged an attack dog. His *Incredible Hulk* episode featured the Hulk rescuing a retarded boy from a demolition derby.

"You need to have a sense of what is saleable," he says. "But you have to decide how important that is. You can lose your artistic attitude to sell, say, soap flakes. There's a thin line there, a very thin line between eating and maintaining your integrity."

Jaron Summers lives in Hollywood, where he recently earned $40,000 for scripting an episode of *Miami Vice*.

SEVENTY-NINE

570

GRANVILLE STREET

Although Emily Carr, widely hailed as British Columbia's most original painter, was based primarily in Victoria, her first studio was here on Granville Street. Carr was also an exceptionally talented writer whose connections with Vancouver (particularly Ira Dilworth, regional head of the CBC, and Garnet Sedgewick, head of the UBC English Department, after whom UBC's Sedgewick Library is named) were essential to the development of a literary career. Although Emily Carr was never a fiction writer, much of her work is mistakenly perceived as fiction.

Emily Carr was born in Victoria in 1871. Her mother died, probably of tuberculosis, in 1886. Her father died, of a lung hemorrhage in 1888, leaving five daughters and one son an estate valued at $50,000. She left to study painting in San Francisco for three years in 1891, and travelled to England to study in 1899. In January of 1903 she was admitted to the East Anglia

Sanitarium for treatment of "hysteria" and remained there until March, 1904. She returned home to Victoria via the Cariboo.

In January of 1906 Emily Carr came to live for four-and-a-half years in Vancouver. She had accepted a part-time position as an instructor to a group she refers to in her memoirs as the Vancouver Ladies' Art Club. She initially lived on Melville Street with a niece who had married Frank Boultbee. The teaching job lasted one month before Carr's impatience with the hobbyists ("middle-age society dames") caused a rift. She then took two rooms on the second floor of the Fee Block, a new stone building at 570 Granville, between Dunsmuir and Pender. She placed an ad in the *News-Advertiser*: "Miss M. Emily Carr, Classes in Drawing and Painting, Studio Room 6, Fee Block, next to the Bank of Montreal, Granville Street." By the end of 1907 she had approximately seventy-five students. She lived in a variety of boarding houses in Vancouver during this period: Mrs. Frame's Oakes on Burrard, Mrs. Baker's Tea Kettle Inn on Dunsmuir and a large house at 1935 Granville. By 1909 she was able to invest in five city lots in a new Rosedale Hastings Townsite subdivision.

In her painting trips to Stanley Park, the "appalling solemnity, majesty and silence was the Holiest thing I ever felt." Frequently quarrelsome, she developed a deep friendship with Sophie Frank, a Squamish Indian whom Carr frequently visited at the North Vancouver Reserve, resulting in Carr's oft-anthologized prose piece, "Sophie," from *Klee Wyck*.

At age sixty-nine, Carr published nineteen Indian stories in *Klee Wyck*, "for the pure joy of reliving and travelling among the places and people I love." In 1941 the first printing of 2,500 copies almost sold out by Christmas. Critics such as Robertson Davies praised her style, her distinctly British Columbian material and "her clear, powerful, original and rigorous mind." This first book was initially to be called *Stories in Cedar* but was changed to *Klee Wyck*, a name Indians of Ucluelet had given Carr, on her sketching expeditions, meaning "Laughing One." This slim memoir of Indians she had encountered in such remote locales as the Skeena River, the Nass River and the Queen Charlotte Islands, earned Emily Carr a Governor General's Award in 1942. Emily Carr became the first British Columbian to earn the nation's highest literary honour along with Anne Marriott, who won the Governor General's Award for poetry in the same year.

In her posthumously published *Growing Pains: The Autobiography of Emily Carr* (1971), the author, at age seventy, says, "I would rather have the good-will and kind wishes of my home town, the people I have lived among all my life, than the praise of the whole world." Nonetheless, her third collection, *The House of All*

Sorts (1944), about her experiences as an eccentric Victoria landlady, contains numerous venomous portraits of her former tenants, written in the spirit of revenge. Her second collection, *The Book of Small* (1942), contains reminiscences of childhood. Other books of anecdotes and journals have been published posthumously.

Emily Carr's lengthiest period of residence in Vancouver, managing her Granville Street studio, were some of the happiest years of her life, filled, in her own words, with "joy, independence and lots of laughing." Vancouver was mostly important to Carr in her later years as the home of her closest and most loyal friend, Ira Dilworth, her literary editor and advisor, with whom she exchanged rings and to whom she bequeathed "all my manuscripts and all the books written by me belonging to me at my death in respect of such of my manuscripts or books written by me and published in my lifetime." Ira Dilworth died in 1962. A collection of Carr's autobiographical sketches, *Hundreds and Thousands*, appeared in 1966.

The Vancouver Art Gallery owns the largest collection of Emily Carr's art and maintains a permanent Emily Carr exhibition on its main floor. There is also a park in West Vancouver called Klee Wyck to honour her as a painter. Carr's sister Alice had a bridge constructed in Victoria's Beacon Hill Park in memory of Emily, Carr's Victoria home is preserved as an historic site, and Emily Carr lies buried in Victoria's Ross Bay Cemetery, only a few miles from the painter's much loved Dallas Road cliffs. Carr bequeathed her paints, brushes and unused canvases to the Nootka artist George Clutesi, who is also a published writer.

EIGHTY

817

GRANVILLE STREET

For twenty-six years, in Suite Twelve of this building, which still stands in 1986, Allen Roy Evans operated the Canadian Writers Service, marketing editorial advice to aspiring writers.

Allen Roy Evans was born in Napanee, Ontario in 1885. He grew up in Napinka and Winnipeg in Manitoba. He studied literature at the Universities of Manitoba and Chicago and at Columbia University. He taught English in Vancouver high schools before turning to journalism. His first novel, *Reindeer Trek* (1935), was remarkable in subject matter, well-written and a financial success. It's the story of the unprecedented effort to drive 3,000 reindeer along the northeastern coast of Alaska into northern Canada. In 1929 the Canadian government purchased the reindeer from the Lomen Reindeer Corporation of Alaska to replace the dwindling caribou herds as a food supply for Eskimos. Andrew Bahr, a Laplander, with a dozen Lapland and Eskimo assistants, completed the gruelling 2,000-mile journey five years later. Evans' novel recounts the hardships that befell the herders. A year after the book's publication he established his Evans National School for Writers at 1200 Nicola, which he moved to 1538 Beach Avenue in 1938. His school became the Canadian Writers Service on Granville Street in 1939, where it remained until Evans' eightieth year in 1965. His other novel, much less successful, is *All in a Twilight*, a biographically based study of his parents' difficulties as a pioneer couple on the Prairies.

EIGHTY-ONE

Binky's Oyster Bar

784 THURLOW

Named in honour of the beloved, eccentric leftist Binky Marks, who for many years seemingly-haphazardly but intelligently managed Duthie Books Paperbackcellar (where most writers buy books in Vancouver, and which is now managed by David Kerfoot), the distinctly un-Binky Marks-like New Orleans-styled oyster bar and restaurant, operated by Nick Hunt and Celia Duthie, is avoided by some writers and equally attractive to many others such as novelist and United Church minister Thomas York.

Thomas York was born on November 21, 1940 in Washington, DC. He spent his childhood and youth in Little Rock, Arkansas. He first came to Vancouver in 1967 and slept in Stanley Park. "We were awakened by squirrels skittering, then a cougar bounding over us, literally. We de-camped to the beach and were deluged before dawn by the tide coming in. My first experience of tides, cougars and Vancouver."

From 1967 to 1970 he served as a minister in the Queen Charlotte Islands and Bella Bella, spending his summers in Vancouver where he researched his Ph.D. dissertation on Malcolm Lowry at UBC's Special Collections reading room. He became a Canadian citizen in 1970. From 1982 to 1985 he lived in Pemberton, BC but often visited Vancouver. "Binky's has become my hang-out when I am in Vancouver.

Anyone I want to see—other writers, UBC or SFU profs, serious readers, opera lovers, even trappers and grizzly hunters from the north—frequent Binky's. Vancouver has become, in effect, my city, as Toronto was before it, and New Orleans before that. To me it's a small town, not a big city. That's part of its appeal. The other part is that it is incomparably beautiful. I can be in Vancouver and still be a nature mystic."

Thomas York's novels are *We, the Wilderness* (1973), *Snowman* (1976), *The Musk Ox Passion* (1978) and *Trapper* (1981). He has also published an autobiography, *And Sleep in the Woods* (1978).

EIGHTY-TWO

MacMillian Bloedel

1075 WEST GEORGIA

The co-founder of the largest company in the province's chief industry, forestry, is commemorated by this cement office tower and by Mazo de la Roche's novel, *Growth of a Man* (1938).

As the fictionalized biography of H.R. MacMillan's early years up to his marriage and permanent residency in BC, *Growth of a Man* recounts the rearing of Shaw Manifold, "that little boy no one had wanted," by stern grandparents. The youth perseveres, studies forestry in Ontario, and comes to BC from Ottawa to be head of the "Department of Forestry in the West." De la Roche was a personal friend of H.R. MacMillan and writes, "He was going to devote his life to the protection of the forest, to the planning of new forests. He was the bridegroom, he thought, of the forest...." The partnership with Bloedel is hinted at when Shaw Manifold, newly married, is on an ocean liner at the end of the novel for "a world tour of investigation of the subject of forestry." He recalls a conversation with a man who wanted a partner in the lumber business. "The man had money but he wanted a partner who knew the forests, who had a complete knowledge of the forest land of British Columbia, and who knew when and where trees should be cut."

Mazo de la Roche was born in Toronto in 1879. She became Canada's best known novelist with her sixteen *Jalna* novels of Upper Canadian life. These have reputedly sold over eleven million copies and remain in print. *Growth of a Man* fits into her attractive myth of a humane and harmless gentry. She died in 1961.

EIGHTY-THREE

Holiday Inn

1133 W. HASTINGS

In the revolving dining room atop the Holiday Inn, Vancouver parole officer Dr. Martin Stanley Ellis confides his intention to mastermind the train robbery of "The Canadian" to his first of three accomplices, Charlie Webb, a small-time boxing promoter, in Tony Foster's thriller *The Money Burn* (1984).

Tony Foster was born in Winnipeg in 1932. After a less than successful scholastic career involving seventeen schools, he joined the RCAF at age seventeen. He has been a merchant seaman, bush pilot and gun runner. He has been jailed in Latin America "for being a capitalist" and jailed eight months in California for drug smuggling. He received a degree in economics from the University of Mexico. His first two novels are *Zig Zag to Armageddon* and *By-pass*. He lives in Halifax with his wife and family.

Foster's third novel, *The Money Burn*, occurs mostly in Vancouver, and is inspired by an actual train robbery attempt in the early 1970s. Dr. Ellis successfully robs the train carrying old paper money across the country to the Royal Mint in Ottawa to be burned, then "burns" his accomplices on parole by saying the banks had already drilled perforations in the stolen bills (secured safely in the walls of the camper he has left parked in Grand Rapids, Michigan). Most of the novel concerns the organization of the heist from Vancouver. Ellis lives in Surrey. Penny Warren, "a gorgeous blonde thirsty for revenge against the system," lives in West Van. Colin McCurdy, an ex-drug running pilot, keeps his seaplane in Ladner (and develops a love interest with Warren). Charlie Webb is killed in a shoot-out during the robbery in Sault Ste. Marie.

EIGHTY-FOUR

Canada Place

Formerly the site of CPR #6 shed, here **Jack London** at age eighteen ended his days as a hobo by boarding the steamship *Umatilla* to return to San Francisco. He had left Oakland in April of 1894 and kept a "Tramp Diary" which resulted in *The Road* (1907). London recalls hopping freights across Canada and arriving in Vancouver in 1896 in a story called "Hobos That Pass in the Night." He stayed in Vancouver for a week. According to Russell Kingsman's *A Pictorial Life of Jack London*, "Vancouver was a perfect ending for Jack's life as a tramp and would always be a fond memory." He begged door-to-door and was only refused twice, both times because he arrived after dinner. Even then he was apparently given money to make up for the refusal of food.

Although he never visited Vancouver, **Jules Verne**'s two volume adventure novel, *Le Volcan d'Or* (1906) is partially set in Vancouver. Part one of the novel was reissued in 1962 in English as *The Claim on Forty Mile Creek*.

EIGHTY-FIVE

The Felix Apartments

610 JERVIS STREET (JERVIS AND PENDER)

A.M. Stephen

Here, in Suite 41, lived A.M. Stephen, the greatest humanitarian of all Vancouver writers, whose exemplary life and writing have been under-valued and under-recognized by the city.

Alexander Maitland Stephen, the social activist and author, known to his friends as A.M., was born in Hanover, Ontario in 1882. His parents were both of aristocratic Scottish ancestry. They moved to Victoria, BC in 1898 where their son articled with his uncle's law firm at age sixteen. Disenchanted with the majesty of the law and possessed with a socialist impatience, Stephen abandoned a career in law after one year in order to prospect for gold in the Klondike. He punched cattle in Alberta, worked as a guide in the Rockies and taught school at Rock Creek, BC in 1906. Never greatly attracted to money, he reputedly turned down a promotion in Victoria selling life insurance for $300 a month in order to take a $1-a-day cow-punching job. He worked briefly as a logger in Oregon in 1910. His studies in architecture at the University of Chicago until 1913 took him overseas to England where he enlisted in 1914. He was injured in France and returned to Vancouver with a shattered right wrist, virtually penniless, in 1918, to open a structural engineering firm.

His crusading spirit for social reform led him to form the Child Welfare Association. Convinced that "in child welfare lay the welfare of all the world," his

125

Association was instrumental in establishing the Mother's Pension Act, the Minimum Wage Act, divorce law amendments and improved social services for destitute and handicapped children. As an essayist Stephen proposed more frank attitudes to sexuality and supported female emancipation ("Woman has rebelled, and rightly so, at the double standard, that she has been subjected to.")

Turning to teaching, Stephen agitated for numerous reforms, most of which were implemented after his dismissal for insubordination. "The central principle of our graded system," he claimed, "is that the child must fit the school and not the school must fit the child." He turned to his pen for his living, becoming associate editor of the *Western Tribune*, a leftist weekly. His popularity as a public speaker reputedly caused him to move from Dundarave in West Vancouver to Vancouver. In 1924 he lived at suite 27 in the Manhatten Apartments at 784 Thurlow (a building that still stands).

A great admirer of Swinburne, Stephen published his first successful book of poetry, *The Rosary of Pan*, in 1923. After editing two school anthologies, *The Voice of Canada* (1926), and *The Golden Treasury of Canadian Verse* (1927), and issuing a second acclaimed poetry collection, *The Land of the Singing Waters* (1927), Stephen's literary reputation was firmly established across Canada.

A.M. Stephen's first novel, *The Kingdom of the Sun* (1927), was a strange historical romance about a gentleman adventurer named Richard Anson, who sailed aboard Sir Francis Drake's *Golden Hind*, only to be cast away amongst the Haida natives. Anson's love interest is a golden-haired princess, Auria, reared by the Haida to serve as an ethereal princess. Auria must choose between earthly affection and mystical duties. The novel is drawn from legendary evidence that fair-haired individuals did occasionally and unaccountably appear among the Haida.

In *The Gleaming Archway* (1929), one of the first of numerous novels from British Columbia to feature disaffected male journalists, Vancouver is referred to as the Mystic City and the City Beautiful. A.M. Stephen, himself a Vancouver newspaperman, has a fictional prototype in the novel, Craig Maitland, who is a dreamer in the twin realms of love and politics:

"To Craig Maitland, standing upon the edge of Grouse Mountain plateau, it seemed that he had paused for a moment upon the brink of some dream world which was built of the aerie substance of imagination— a perishable palace of beauty wrought of star-dust and moonbeams...Only when one looked towards the city, which lay like an aeroplane map unrolled to southward,

A.M. Stephen

did one realise Man, the microcosm, had entered and had changed this universe of the Titans and had placed these puny structures in contrast with nature."

As a moderate socialist, Maitland takes a respite from the restrictions of a journalism career and holidays in the rough 'n tumble Squamish Valley amongst radical "reds," Indians and expatriate English eccentrics. He befriends a Marxist publisher, a Russian revolutionary and a beautiful Englishwoman. He also meets a brutish, volatile leftist named Bud Powers, who proves to be his nemesis as the symbolic representation of the primitive elements of man's nature that invariably scuttle social progress.

Unlucky in love (Jocelyn, the Englishwoman, is married), Maitland returns to Vancouver to ardently assist in the publication of the *Beacon*, a socialist weekly headquartered on Pender Street. He forms a sentimental friendship with emancipated colleague, Madge, atop Grouse Mountain and in Capilano Canyon, but impulsively marries Shannon, a painted lady with a heart of gold whom he meets in a Chinatown gambling house.

Eventually, the gleaming archways of Craig Maitland's idealistic spirit come crashing down to earth and he accepts an invitation to leave on a treasure hunting expedition in the South Seas, unaware that his friends have arranged for him to be reunited with his first true love, Jocelyn, whose husband has since conveniently died.

Stephen believed that "authentic poetry, in whatever genre it happens to be, is always better than the best prose." As an active member of the Vancouver Poetry Society, he eventually formed a Vancouver chapter of the League of Western Writers in 1931. A reviewer in the *Vancouver Sun* wrote, "I think that A.M. Stephen is the Canadian Carl Sandburg, the logical successor to Bliss Carman as *the* poet of the country. I think he's a genius." His much anthologized poem of tribute, "Vancouver," was printed in the *Sunday Province* on October 1, 1934. He published two other poetry books in his lifetime, *Brown Earth and Bunch Grass* (1932) and an epic lyric titled *Verendrye* (1935). He had close personal ties with Bliss Carman and Sir Charles G.D. Roberts.

Stephen the activist used his literary stature to promote his social concerns after the demise of the *Western Tribune* in 1929 because of the Depression. As a member of the Progressive Film Association, the Vancouver Art Gallery, president of the Vancouver Lodge of the Theosophical Society and a highly respected critic of his times, Stephen successfully launched the BC branch of the League Against War and Fascism. He stood as a candidate for the CCF in the

Alberni-Nanaimo riding and was narrowly defeated. He was later expelled from the CCF for advocating a popular front with the Communists.

He corresponded with Norman Bethune, raised funds for China and wrote numerous pamphlets analysing global politics from a leftist perspective. Possibly Stephen's radicalism was tempered by the violent RCMP actions in Regina during the great trek of the unemployed to Ottawa. His second son, Leslie (born in 1914) was helping at his cousin's ranch for the summer in Saskatchewan. In Regina to buy grain for seeding, Leslie Stephen was caught in the riot and so brutally beaten on the head by police that he was made an invalid for life.

A.M. Stephen succumbed to pneumonia complications at St. Paul's Hospital on Dominion Day, 1942. Wreaths were sent by such diverse groups as the Chinese Benevolent Association and the Boilermakers and Iron Shipbuilders Union. His wife arranged for a collection of posthumous poetry, *Songs for a New Nation* (1963).

Gordon Stephen, the younger brother of A.M. Stephen, was the most influential publishing presence in BC for most of the century. From 1927 until 1961 he was western manager for the English firm of J.M. Dent & Sons, building the largest textbook and publishing business in western Canada. After his brother had published two books with Dent, Gordon Stephen persuaded the company to open a Vancouver office in an old mansion at Robson and Jervis. This office was called Aldine House in accordance with Dent & Sons tradition. All Dent offices were called Aldine, after the medieval printer, Aldous.

Gordon Stephen died November 30, 1961 at the age of seventy-three. Aldine House was demolished the following year. In her memoirs, poet Dorothy Livesay has noted the Stephen brothers were very different. "Gordon, all through the Depression, remained very 'square' and establishment," she writes, "but 'A.M.' as he was fondly called, had become radicalized."

EIGHTY-SIX

The Bayshore Inn

1601 WEST GEORGIA

Hammond Innes' *High Stand* (1985) culminates with a romantic tryst in the Bayshore after the couple dines at the nearby Coal Harbour Keg restaurant.

Ralph Innes, known professionally for over half a century as **Hammond Innes**, was born a Scot in England in 1913. He has achieved international success as an author of adventure novels as well as with a fictionalized account of Captain Cook's final voyage. An experienced seaman and traveller, Innes has been visiting Canada since the early 1950s. For many years Innes and his playwright wife, who reside in Suffolk, have taken to planting Canadian trees in Wales. "As they grow into tall timber," he writes, "they give me an increasing sense of achievement and satisfaction...I have for a long time wanted to write a novel that, at least in part, was about trees...*High Stand* is the result."

High Stand is Innes' twenty-ninth book and the fourth with a Canadian setting. It is the story of Philip Redfern, a young solicitor, who must travel to a Yukon gold mine owned by a client. The client has disappeared and changed his will to disenfranchise his wife, Miriam. Redfern flies Wardair to the BC coast. "There was a marvellous view of Vancouver sitting like a miniature Manhattan surrounded by vast expanses of sunbright water." After much intrigue and treachery in the Yukon and down the Inside Passage, Redfern discovers his own manliness and develops a love interest in Miriam. "Sex in the wilderness," maintains Innes, who researched *High Stand* in BC in 1982, "is a natural aspect of a man's and a woman's relationship as they struggle against the environment. Sex for the sake of sex is a city thing." In some respects *High Stand*, which shows Innes' appreciation for what he refers to as "outback" Canadians, is similar to the romantic English adventure thrillers of writers such as Harold Bindloss and Robert Allison Hood in the early twentieth century—life in the de-civilized colonies encourages a man's virility, the hero safeguards justice, then he gets the girl. Philip Redfern and Miriam reunite on the final pages and wake together in the Bayshore "with the hills upside down in the flat mirror of Burrard Inlet" and the future before them.

EIGHTY-SEVEN

The Lions

The snow-capped twin peaks on the North Shore have long captured the fancy of camera-toting tourists and impressionable writers. The first author to co-opt the Lions for literary purposes was D.W. Higgins, whose second book, *The Passing of a Race and More Tales of*

Western Life (1904), featured the Lions on the cover and contained a chapter called "The Lions." (The Lions have since lent their name to a suspension bridge built by a British liquor corporation in order to develop the British Properties in West Vancouver and to a professional sports franchise that sells American-style football.)

David William Higgins was born in Halifax, Nova Scotia on November 30, 1834. His father had emigrated from Manchester in 1814. He was raised and educated in New York. In 1856 he went to San Francisco where he edited and partly owned a newspaper, *Morning Call*. He sold his interests in 1858 to search for gold in the Cariboo region of BC. ("The country now known as British Columbia was then named New Caledonia. It was a wild and trackless section, inhabited by numerous tribes of savage red men, who were controlled and held in check with difficulty by the wise policy of the Hudson's Bay Co., the nominal rulers.")

David William Higgins

After prospecting he worked for two and a half years as a reporter on the *Colonist* in Victoria. He left to start the *Chronicle* newspaper which was then absorbed by the *Colonist*. He was editor of the *Colonist* for twenty-four years and took part in the negotiations whereby British Columbia entered Confederation. He became a politician and served as Speaker of the BC Legislature from 1890 to 1898. His two books of "history in an entertaining manner," *The Mystic Spring and Other Tales of Western Life* (1904) and *The Passing of a Race*, fancifully depict colourful anecdotes and characters on the West Coast in the latter half of the 19th century.

In "The Lions" Higgins describes, "those wonderful carvings from the workshop of Nature which challenge the admiration and excite in all beholders a feeling of awe, as high up in the mountains at the entrance to Burrard Inlet they crouch like huge sentinels keeping watch and ward over the gateway through which is destined to pass the commerce of our mighty Empire." The vague storyline recalls the Great Fire of June 13th, 1886 and concludes, "The Lions remain faithful to their trust. Day following day finds them grim, watchful and incorruptible, presiding in silent majesty over the western gateway of the Dominion. And so will they continue to guard countless generations of men as they come and go, until heaven and earth shall be rolled up like a scroll, and there will be no more sea."

D.W. Higgins also wrote editorials for the *Vancouver World* after his retirement. "The oldest newspaperman on the coast" died on his 83rd birthday, on November 30, 1917.

Another newspaperman who wrote novels is Dick

Diespecker. In his 1953 novel, *Rebound*, he describes Prospect Point in Stanley Park:

"He walked on past the old Indian shacks and the carved bowsprit of the Empress of Japan, past the Lumberman's Arch and up the long winding road through heavy timber until he came out upon the peak of Prospect Point. He walked down to the lookout below the signal station and stared down two hundred feet to the swirling, uneasy waters of the Narrows.

"Here was loneliness made more alone. He was like an ant upon a vast desert, a bobbing cork upon the limitless ocean, a speck of infinity. Above him the eternity of space, around him the blackness of night, pierced only by the cold stars, light-years removed, and the winking of the lighthouse at Point Atkinson. Alone, solitary and engulfed by sorrow, lost in the enormous well of hatred."

Dick Diespecker was born at Adstock, Bucks, England. He was educated at Pretoria and Capetown, South Africa. His family moved to Victoria, BC where he published his first poem in the *Daily Colonist* at age fifteen. He began his newspaper career as a reporter for the *Vancouver Star* in 1927, worked in advertising, and joined CJOR radio at 846 Howe Street in 1936 as a playwright, news commentator and producer. He wrote over 400 radio dramas, some of which were broadcast internationally. During World War II he served with the Royal Canadian Artillery and as Radio Liaison Officer in Ottawa and overseas. His "Prayer for Victory," written in a Montreal hotel room in 1942, was aired on networks throughout the western world. He published his first collection of poems, *Between Two Furious Oceans*, in 1944, and resumed residency in Vancouver.

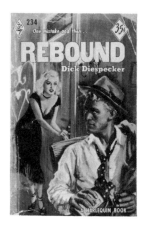

Diespecker worked for CJOR from 1945 to 1949, living at 1140 W. Pender. In 1950 he published his first novel, *Elizabeth*, a weak biographical novel about a South-African-born woman's journey through life, from the land of Diespecker's own roots to England and finally to Victoria, BC. In 1950 he also began working for the *Province* as radio director and remained as promotions manager until 1956. During this period he lived at 2804 W. 15th and at 3507 Puget Street.

Diespecker's second and far superior novel, *Rebound*, is the story of Stoney Martin, a Vancouver journalist who, in 1950, is returning to Vancouver from Toronto by train with his second wife, Jane. By coincidence, his conniving first wife. Susan, is also on the train. As the train makes its way across Canada, Stoney reminisces, recalling his stormy relationship with the "predatory female" who tricked him with a false pregnancy into a miserable marriage.

The novel paints an excellent picture of post-Depression Vancouver—there is a particularly effective scene in which Stoney looks down upon the Victory Square cenotaph from his newspaper office on the eve of the outbreak of World War II. When *Rebound* is not exonerating Stoney's part in his sexual relationship with the relentlessly "bad" Susan, it is a fine novel with clear-eyed accounts of social problems and a deep sensitivity to Vancouver's unique character. Unfortunately the book was packaged as a potboiler of contemporary passions and Diespecker's strength as a social critic is submerged.

EIGHTY-EIGHT

Lions Gate Bridge

Bruce McKelvie

In B.A. McKelvie's collection of five Indian tales, *Legends of Stanley Park* (1941), he claims this site was the home of Si'atmulth, the Rainmaker. Si'atmulth punishes Chief Kapalana of the nearby Squamish village by imposing a severe drought upon the World, whereupon the Insect People assault Si'atmulth's house and steal his baby. Si'atmulth is forced to make peace with Kapalana. "And that is why," concludes McKelvie, "when the rain is falling in and about Vancouver, wise old Indians look toward Stanley Park and say, 'Si'atmulth is keeping to his bargain.' "

Bruce Alistair McKelvie was born in BC in 1890. His interest in Indian culture and BC history began early when his family moved to various locales throughout the province. At age ten he worked as a printer's assistant and later wrote for the *Vancouver Province* for over thirty years and for the *Victoria Colonist* for seven years. He retired to Cobble Hill on Vancouver Island where he died in 1960. Mount McKelvie and McKelvie Creek are named in his honour. He wrote several historical books and a teen adventure novel entitled *The Black Canyon* (1958), but is best remembered for his strange first novel, *Huldowget* (1926).

Huldowget is the first BC novel to attempt a depiction of the clash of values between Christianity and native spirituality. At a small mission up the coast called Fort Oliver, Father David, a didactic missionary with forty years experience, learns a half-breed shaman named Thompson is practicing heathen rites. The self-serving Thompson wants to wed Father David's lovely missionary hospital assistant Mary Cunningham who, in turn, loves a local police officer named John Collishaw. Mary falls temporarily under the spell of the "necromancer." The climax occurs when the Indians force Thompson and Collishaw to undergo "trial by mouse" where the tiny animal's movement towards one or the other determines who is to be burned alive. Although *Huldowget* is fanciful to an extreme and condescendingly sympathetic to its Indian characters, it is nonetheless a well-intentioned effort to translate some complex frictions.

EIGHTY-NINE

Lions Gate

"Her high heels clanked on the steel of the empty bridge...She dropped the empty match folder over the side, and it flipped out of sight...She arrived at the middle of the bridge, the highest part...She leaned against the tubular rail and looked into the fog..." The heroine of George Bowering's first novel, *Mirror on the Floor* (1967), doesn't jump. She kills her mother and ends up in Crease Clinic.

Between this sensational ending and the novel's confusing start, *Mirror on the Floor* is an engagingly written and distinctly Vancouver-ish story of one summer in the life of a graduate student named Bob Small. He meets Andrea outside the Vancouver police station on Main Street, falls in love and is shaken from his cryptic, cocky, university-educated self. Alternating storylines from chapter to chapter converge into the novel's convincing love affair. The story is studded with Vancouver landmarks and, more than any other work of fiction by George Bowering, succeeds in making the reader care a great deal about the fates of the central characters.

George Bowering, the best and brightest of the UBC *Tish* movement, was born in 1935 in Penticton. He grew up in the Okanagan Valley and worked as an RCAF aerial photographer after high school, then attended UBC where his M.A. thesis advisor was visiting American poet Robert Creeley. The influx of writers such as Creeley, Robert Duncan and Charles Olson, who were associated with Black Mountain College in North Carolina, profoundly influenced the development of Bowering and his UBC writing colleagues such as Fred Wah, Frank Davey, Lionel Kearns, Daphne Marlatt, James Reid, David Dawson and Dan McLeod. With the encouragement of UBC's Warren Tallman, Bowering and his friends founded a mimeographed magazine called *Tish* in 1961. Bowering and Frank Davey became the leading theorists for a

George Bowering

sophisticated, inward-looking and exclusive school of "post modern" writing (marked by a disdain for "anecdotal nostalgia" in prose and a belief that poets can best use language as an act of discovery rather than an imposition of order). The first nineteen issues of *Tish* have been reprinted by Talonbooks as *Tish 1-19* (1975). Post-modernist prejudices continue to be influential, as many of the radical Tish period writers now teach at universities.

Bowering taught at the University of Calgary and Sir George Williams University and currently teaches at Simon Fraser University. He lives in Kerrisdale. His range as a humourist, critic, theorist, poet and idiosyncratic prose stylist is remarkable. His improvisational wit is frequently brilliant. Some of his pronouncements on writing ("Straight talk does not work in poetry because there are no straight lines in the universe") are pompous, but many more are penetrating and original ("A question of home is the most often encountered theme in British Columbia writing").

His mental agility as Vancouver's Edison of post-modernism is most attractively packaged in his short story collections, *Flycatcher and Other Stories* (1974), *Protective Footwear* (1978) and *A Place to Die* (1983). He won the Governor General's Award for poetry in 1969 with *Rocky Mountain Foot* (1968) and *The Gangs of Kosmos* (1969). His other poetry books include *Points on the Grid* (1964), *The Man in Yellow Boots* (1965), *The Silver Wire* (1967), *Two Police Poems* (1968), *Sitting in Mexico* (1970), *Touch: Selected Poems* (1971), *Autobiology* (1972), *Selected Poems: Particular Accidents* (1980), *West Window* (1982) and *Kerrisdale Elegies* (1984).

In prose, Bowering has moved deliberately from the conventionality and sentimentality of *Mirror on the Floor* to self-conscious experimentation, using prose as a forum for haphazard insights, continually undercutting the facade of realism in storytelling. *A Short Sad Book* (1977) is a pastiche of social commentary ("Canada is the country in which writing about history is history") and playful self-mockery. *Burning Water* (1980), which won a Governor General's Award, features an intrusive author commenting on his own relations to a novel he is writing about Captain George Vancouver's search for the Northwest Passage.

NINETY

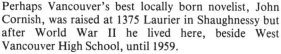

INGLEWOOD AVENUE, WEST VANCOUVER

Perhaps Vancouver's best locally born novelist, John Cornish, was raised at 1375 Laurier in Shaughnessy but after World War II he lived here, beside West Vancouver High School, until 1959.

John Buckley Cornish was born in Vancouver on August 6, 1914. He was the son of Edgar Osman Cornish, manager of Simpson, Roberts & Co., an import-export firm, and Mary (Grierson) Mansell Cornish. He was the editor of the *Ubyssey* in 1935-36, with staffers Norman Depoe and Dorwin Baird, receiving a B.A. in English that same year. He joined the army as a private in 1939. In England he lost the use of one eye in a hand grenade explosion during a training exercise. He continued to serve with the Medical Corps until 1945, when he returned to Vancouver to work as a claims officer with the Unemployment Insurance Commission until 1947. From 1947 until 1952 he worked as a clerk in the Toronto Post Office at night, while writing *The Provincials* during the day.

The Provincials (1951) is a rarity in BC fiction—a delightfully urbane novel that characterizes the economic elite of Vancouver. With a witty stand-offish charm, similar to the satirical style of typically British writers such as Evelyn Waugh, Cornish sets out to recount the relations of an autobiographical narrator, Kenneth Menzies, with the monied Dunseith clan who have secured their fortune in BC's lumber industry. Menzies meets the Dunseith children at an Okanagan private school and is invited to the Dunseith's synthetic baronial Vancouver mansion and the family's summer retreat at Qualicum Beach. " 'Canadians!' laughs Mr. Dunseith. 'You don't know what Canadians are. Nobody knows, not even Ottawa knows. I think Canadians may be like me and I know what I am. I'm a Scotsman resisting becoming an American.' " Mrs. Dunseith hosts cultural events in her home.

The Provincials is about Kenneth Menzies' twenty-year marriage to the entire Dunseith family. The strength of the novel, beyond its extremely clever dialogue and satire, is the narrator's affection and respect for the Dunseiths. He sees them for what they are, and he likes them anyway. The Dunseiths are no better and no worse than the disgruntled unemployed to whom Mayor Gerry McGeer read the Riot Act in 1935. The Dunseiths are, however, rich and they wield power.

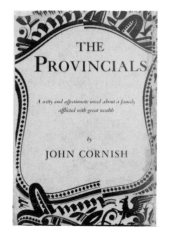

THE
PROVINCIALS

*A witty and affectionate novel about a family
afflicted with great wealth*

by

JOHN CORNISH

The emotionally neutral narrator finds them fascinating. So does the reader. *The Provincials* is one of the most readable, valuable and atypical novels ever written about Vancouver.

The Provincials draws heavily on real BC personalities and owes much of its authenticity to Cornish's prep school education in Vernon and his upper class connections made at Shawnigan Lake Private School. Cornish later claimed he "only wrote *The Provincials* to learn how to playwrite." Returning to live with his widowed mother in 1952, he won a $5,000 *Maclean's* magazine novel-writing contest in 1956 for a slightly bawdy romance about a Doukhobor girl in the BC interior. This novel, *Olga* (1959), was subsequently published but Cornish later regretted the book. It was less successful than *The Provincials*, which had sold 3,500 copies.

Cornish published short stories in Canada and Britain. His next novel, *Sherbourne Street*, (1968) is set in Toronto in the aftermath of World War II when the overflow population lived in trailer camps. In this comic novel Isabel Bailey and her husband, a viola player, plan to re-open a music conservatory with their low-paid, impractical friends. Unfortunately, the music conservatory has become the hope of Isabel's old uncle and his domineering ninety-year-old housekeeper, and their efforts fail. *A World Turned Turtle* (1969) is a tragedy written prior to *Sherbourne Street*, which questions whether a soldier's first loyalty is to the military or humanity. A Canadian military policeman in London during World War II tries to protect his old Estonian math teacher from deportation.

In a 1970 interview John Cornish told *Vancouver Sun* book critic Donald Stainsby, "I suppose I felt British until about 1950. There have always been people who were Canadian, but until the Second World War they were a minority, in BC anyway. When I grew up, England and the US were real and Canada was just where I was. I had the colonial mentality, I suppose." Cornish's work has not received much renown. "It seems enough effort to write a book," he once said, "without turning into a circus act to sell it." Cornish returned to Toronto in 1960.

NINETY-ONE

2749

LAWSON AVENUE, WEST VANCOUVER

This was the principal Vancouver address of one of Canada's foremost writers, Alice Munro. She lived here

Alice Munro

with her first husband, bookseller Jim Munro (Munro's Books in Victoria), and their three daughters from September of 1956 until August of 1963. Earlier she had lived at 445 Kings Road in West Van for three years, on Argyle Street in West Van for six months and in a downstairs flat at 1316 Arbutus for eight months. She arrived in Vancouver by train on January 2, 1952, following her marriage. An office she rented above a drug store on the north side of Marine Drive in West Van, in the 2400 block, was where she wrote one of her best short stories, "The Office." Of these Vancouver locales, Munro says, "I wrote desperately in them all."

Alice Munro was born in Wingham, Ontario on July 10, 1931. Her first collection of short stories, *Dance of the Happy Shades* (1968), received the Governor General's Award, as did her fourth book, *Who Do You Think You Are?* (1978). This latter book, under the title of *The Beggar Maid*, was runner-up for the Booker Prize in the UK. Her other acclaimed books are *Lives of Girls and Women* (1971), *Something I've Been Meaning to Tell You* (1974) and *The Moons of Jupiter* (1982). She returned to southwestern Ontario in 1972 and now lives there in the town of Clinton with her second husband.

West Vancouver is also important for another highly sophisticated writer, Dr. Thomas P. Millar, a child psychologist whose counselling and publishing head-quarters for Palmer Press are at 659 Clyde. Millar is a best-selling non-fiction author on psychology and his novel, *Who's Afraid of Sigmund Freud* (Palmer Press, 1985), was short-listed for the Stephen Leacock Award for Humour. It illustrates the foolishness of assuming that Freudian theories are ultimate and pervasive truths.

NINETY-TWO

Federal Fisheries

4160 MARINE DRIVE, WEST VANCOUVER

One of BC's greatest, most unjustly overlooked novelists, Bertrand W. Sinclair, was a commercial fisherman for over thirty years. His best known novel, *Poor Man's Rock*, realistically depicts the struggle of an independent and impoverished fisherman to combat the industrial stranglehold enjoyed by packing and canning companies, such as Gosse-Millerd Packing Co., in 1918. For many decades a major cannery owned by Francis Millerd was situated at the present site of the federal fisheries base in West Vancouver.

Bertrand W. Sinclair

Bertrand W. Sinclair (a cousin of Upton Sinclair) was born January 9, 1881 in Edinburgh, Scotland. He came to Regina, Saskatchewan in 1889 with his mother, lived in Alberta and ran away from home at age fourteen to become a cowboy in Montana, where he befriended painter Charles Russell and female writer B.M. Bower. Bower and Sinclair collaborated on a temporarily successful and archetypically western story, *Chip of the Flying U*. He roamed to San Francisco and subsequently produced Jack London-influenced novels of adventure, *Raw Gold, Land of the Frozen Sun, Wild West, Pirates of the Plains, Gunpowder Lightning* and *North of Fifty-Three*. He visited Vancouver in 1905 and settled in a new house in Fairview where he adapted his mold of melodramatic, heroic fiction to novels of loggers, fishermen and ranchers. *Big Timber* (1916) described the early BC logging industry. *Burned Bridges* (1919) achieved four editions in as many months.

Poor Man's Rock (1920), a Hardyesque romance, reputedly sold 80,000 copies. Based on first hand experience, Sinclair's story of family pride and capitalist exploitation deserves re-publication. The rock referred to in the title is off Lasqueti Island (described in the novel as Squitty Island) and draws its name from swirling currents and dense kelp at its base which prevented large, motorized fishing vessels from approaching and therefore restricted the fishing to hand trollers. "Only a poor man trolled in a rowboat...Poor Man's Rock had given many a man a chance."

Prior to the turn of the century, a pioneer named Don MacRae had tried to elope with his beloved, Bessie Morton. They were overtaken at sea by Bessie's father, her grandfather and a jealous monied suitor named Horace Gower. Sworn to pacifism by his beloved, MacRae was knocked unconscious by Gower's attack with a pike pole. MacRae drifted and was shipwrecked on Squitty Island. Gower married Bessie. For the next thirty years Gower and his wealthy clan waged a silent, economic war on the unlucky MacRae, slowly divesting him of his property by virtue of the Gowers' clout in the Packers Association. In 1918, MacRae's son, Jack, at twenty-four, returns from the World War I front, learns of the long grudge and his subsequent disinheritance, watches his father die and vows to repurchase the family property and "to take a fall out of Horace Gower that would jar the bones of his ancestors."

Jack MacRae, the hero of *Poor Man's Rock*, realizes the Packers Association controls the local fish industry rates and discourages competition by monopolizing cannery sites and pursing licences. He recognizes "the wholesaler stood like a wall between the fishermen and those who ate fish." MacRae competes with Horace

Gower, gains the support of independent fishermen, offers fair prices, scuttles Gower's monopoly and ends special privileges to BC salmon packers. *Poor Man's Rock* ends happily when MacRae ultimately buries the hatchet with Gower Sr. and allows his love for Gower's daughter, Betty, to blossom into a forthcoming marriage with the blessings of Gower, who confesses to his future son-in-law that wealth had never made him happy.

Hidden Places (1922) concerns the romance of Robin Hollister, a facially mutilated and emotionally shattered thirty-one-year-old World War I veteran ("a single speck of human wreckage cast on a far beach by the receding tides of war") and a blind woman named Doris Cleveland who had established a cabin up the coast in Toba Inlet. *The Inverted Pyramid* (1924) was inspired by the failure of the Dominion Trust Co. *Down the Dark Alley* (1935) is a story of rum-running out of the city of Vancouver in the days of prohibition in the US.

Throughout his work, critic and friend Lester Peterson has noted, there is "general disgust for the mere entrepreneur, the man who manipulates but does not actually produce goods or services...Monetary gain must not, in the Sinclair philosophy, be derived by means which destroy beauty or create waste—a creed which led Sinclair to oppose what he recognized, earlier than most, was senseless despoilation of natural resources." Other works were *Room for the Rolling M*, *Both Sides of the Law* and *The Man Who Rode by Himself* (unpublished). His life and work is the subject of a forthcoming study by Betty Keller.

From 1932 until his retirement from commercial fishing at age eighty-seven, Sinclair, residing chiefly in Pender Harbour, BC, eschewed literature except for poems published in the *Fisherman* newspaper and radio broadcasts he made to fishermen on a regular program called *The Sinclair Hour*. He died at age ninety-one in 1972, survived by his wife, Ora, and their daughter, Mrs. Cherry Whitaker. His ashes were scattered at Lasqueti Island.

The captain and crew of *Stalward 2* depart for deep sea fishing adventures as well in W.A. Hagelund's *The Halibut-Hunters* (1963), a novel that provides a detailed look at coastal fishing practices and practitioners. The two central characters are a rough and experienced Captain Alex Hansen, who has lost his son to the sea, and a sixteen-year-old novice seaman, Alan Murray, who has lost his father to the sea. Hansen reluctantly takes Murray into his crew, saying, "Life's always tough on young people; does them a world of good. Show me a kid who has it easy and I'll show you a potential failure." Headed for Sand Point, Alaska, the refurbished vessel encounters environmental and political obstacles and a layover at Prince Rupert. After witnessing his first burial at sea, Alan partakes in a record catch and sails back to Vancouver having earned his manhood.

William A. Hagelund was born in Vancouver. He fished for twelve years on the BC coast, partially as a whaler. After service as a seaman in World War II, he became an engineer but retained his skipper's papers. He was a director of the World Ship Society of Western Canada and authored a book on west coast fishing, *Flying the Chase Flag* (1961).

West Vancouver was also important to the writing career of **Harry Maitland Twigg**, who lived at 1267 Duchess Avenue from 1923–1939. Born in Victoria on February 5, 1901, Twigg published fiction and non-fiction in numerous outdoor magazines. He died at Oyster Bay on Vancouver Island on January 5, 1946.

NINETY-THREE

4715

CAULFEILD PLACE, WEST VANCOUVER

Robert Harlow, one of the most significant novelists native to British Columbia, describes this address, where he lived for five years (1969–1974), as "the geographical centre of all that's rotten in this part of the world for me." He used this former residence as the model of the house owned by his protagonist undergoing mid-life crises in *Paul Nolan*, his fifth novel, which appeared in 1983.

Robert Harlow was born in Prince Rupert on November 19, 1923. He grew up in Prince George, where his father was a roadmaster with the CNR. His first three novels, *Royal Murdoch* (1962), *A Gift of Echoes* (1965) and *Scann* (1972), all centre upon a fictional BC town of Linden, modelled on Prince George. *Scann*, about the local newspaper editor Amory Scann, is a critically acclaimed and complex pastiche of several novellas, in which Amory Scann concludes by burning the manuscript he has been writing to mark the fiftieth anniversary of the town.

Harlow first visited Vancouver in 1941 to join the Air Force. He attended UBC after the war, joining Earle Birney's initial creative writing workshops. He then became the first of many prominent Canadian writers

Robert Harlow

to go to the now prestigious Writers' Workshop at the University of Iowa. From 1953 until 1965 he worked for CBC in Vancouver, becoming regional director of radio programming. He helped Robert Weaver instigate the literary program *Anthology* and aided in the birth of the UBC literary magazine *Prism International*. He became founding head of Canada's first Creative Writing Department at UBC in 1965, remaining in that position until 1976.

Paul Nolan is a brave and engaging work in which Harlow is willing to explore his autobiographical main character at his worst as well as his best, unleashing his sensitive anger with hurtful poise. The dissatisfactions with bourgeois values expressed in *Paul Nolan* were harbingers of Robert Harlow's partial renunciation of Vancouver in 1985:

"I came to Vancouver in 1951 initially for two weeks. Those two weeks are just about up. I'm not sure why I stayed. The best answer I can give at the moment is hope. I hoped a number of things would happen, and I hoped a number of other things wouldn't happen.

"Most people—including myself—begin by writing about Vancouver's scenery. They talk about its pretty setting and how only Hong Kong, Rio, San Francisco and Capetown rival it...Vancouver is a city like any other in most ways, but it is probably more middle class than any other I've known. If you have a home, a boat, a car, skis, a swimming pool, a large garden and a job to support all those things, then there is reason to be a booster. But a paradise for yuppies simply breeds more yuppies.

"We've had them in Vancouver for a long, long time. My grandfather moved to Prince Rupert in 1910 to get away from them. In those days they lived in Shaughnessy and were just as self-centred, self-satisfied and self-important as the ones who live all over the Lower Mainland today. If you're old and poor, young and poor, plain poor or disadvantaged, this is not a welcoming place in which to try to live. It is also young, very young in the head, the kind of young that breeds western apocalyptic paranoia.

"I think I hate the kind of extreme conservatism that reigns in the province of which Vancouver is the commercial centre. It hurts to see what is being done to education, what has, in fact, been done to our forests and our fish, and what has been done to the Fraser Valley. It's crippling for mind and spirit to live in a place that once had more potential than much of the rest of the country put together, and to see it plundered and squandered by a collective conservative mind that believes literally at this date that profit is holy, that the business of business is only business and that it would rather be dead than red. That collective mind does not think uniquely about this place. Instead it sucks up tired tripe from the USA and something called the Fraser Institute. There is no sense of destiny here...

"When all the blame is laid at all the doors possible and there is still blame enough left over to lay at the doors of nearly three million British Columbians, maybe some of those things many of us hoped would happen thirty-five years ago will happen. But I doubt it. I doubt it so much that the struggle to believe in the province I was born in, and the town I've lived and worked in most of my life, is no longer worth it. Going will be sad, but when it happens it will be good."

Harlow's comic novel, *Making Arrangements* (1978), has an interesting history. As a send-up of the Vancouver horseracing world centred in Exhibition Park, the riotous tale narrated by a one-legged "punter" drew uncomfortably close parallels to noted personalities at the track. Political pressure was placed upon the publisher, Jack McClelland, after publication, to bury the book. McClelland, according to Harlow, consented. Involving drugs, the kidnapping of an industrialist and even pay-TV sex, *Making Arrangements* mainly follows the fortunes of some likeable losers who scramble to raise money for a once-in-a-lifetime bet from their headquarters at a seedy downtown hotel. The model for the hotel scenes was the Hotel Austin on Granville Street, before it was refurbished as a trendy strip club. *Making Arrangements* was re-released in paperback in 1985 following the election of a different federal government.

In 1985 Harlow also published *Felice: A Travelogue*, a novel prompted by travels in Poland with his second wife. The novel contains a powerful account of an upsetting visit to Auschwitz by a Vancouver dentist and his wife in striking and purposeful contrast to their privileged life "in the still-life of Point Grey."

NINETY-FOUR

7165

CLIFF ROAD, WEST VANCOUVER

"Jas" Clavell, later better known throughout the world as **James Clavell**, lived here with his wife, April, from 1963 to 1972. He came to live here following the success of *King Rat* (1962), the first novel of his "Asian Saga." *Tai-Pan* (1966) was mostly written in West Vancouver. *Noble House* (1981) earned Clavell a $1-million advance. Vancouver plays a minimal role in *Noble House*, with a reference to Chinatown's "Pedder

James Clavell

June Skinner and sister

Street" on page 1051. *Shogun* (1975) sold 3.5 million copies in paperback, was on the best-seller list for thirty-two weeks and was adapted by Clavell into a twelve-hour mini-series for television.

Clavell has demanded a minimum advance of $3 million for his next novel, *Whirlwind*, which uses some of the characters from *Noble House* but is set in and around Iran in 1979.

June Skinner, the first female novelist born in Vancouver, currently residing in West Vancouver, also saw one of her novels become a movie. Hollywood transformed her third novel, *Let's Kill Uncle* (1965), into a film starring British actor Nigel Greene. "The movie version premiered locally at the drive-in in Vancouver in 1968," remembers Skinner, whose pen name is Rohan O'Grady. "My next door neighbour had a little party and we all drove over from West Van to see it. It was raining so hard we had to put cardboard over the roof just to see the screen. I'd set the book on one of the Gulf Islands and there was a cougar in the story. They'd switched the whole thing to some tropical island off Mexico or Texas. The cougar became a shark. Sometimes I think all they really bought from me was the title. Now I see *Let's Kill Uncle* is on television at 2 a.m. every six months or so."

June Skinner was born in Vancouver on July 23, 1922. Raised in Point Grey, she took business courses and worked at the Capilano Golf and Country Club. She also worked in the library of the *Sun* where she met her husband, newspaperman Fred Skinner. Skinner lived in West Vancouver for twenty-five years, moved to Tsawwassen briefly and returned to West Vancouver in 1986. Her first novel and her favourite, *O'Houlihan's Jest* (1961), required much research into Irish history. Her second, *Pippin's Journal* (1962), was a neo-gothic story republished in Britain as *The Curse of the Montrolfes*.

Let's Kill Uncle drew heavily upon her knowledge of the coastal islands where her father served as provincial forester. *Bleak November* (1967), her least favourite novel, was written at the request of her New York editor, who wanted a fictional account of a sensational Coquitlam murder that had made international head-lines. Discouraged by minimal recognition, rejection slips and slim earnings, Skinner took a hiatus until publishing, under the pseudonym Ann Carleon, *Mayspoon* (1982), a novel based upon her experiences in West Vancouver raising her daughters.

The other world-wide-selling fiction writer with Van-couver connections is Arthur Hailey. The climax of Hailey's first novel, *Flight Into Danger* (1958), features the former terminal facility, now used for private

143

planes, as the destination for a beleaguered commercial aircraft. The plane's passengers and crew are beset by serious outbreaks of food poisoning. Co-authored by John Castle and released a year later in the US as *Runway Zero-Eight*, Hailey's thriller gradually achieved publication in over twenty languages. It was the source of a Paramount feature film titled *Zero Hour*.

Arthur Hailey was born in Luton, England on April 5, 1920. An RAF pilot, he immigrated to Canada in 1947. Now a Canadian citizen living in the Bahamas, the millionaire writer is best known for *In High Places* (1962), *Hotel* (1965), *Airport* (1968) and *Wheels* (1971).

NINETY-FIVE

Horseshoe Bay

WEST VANCOUVER

The pivotal scene in Margaret Walker's comic novel of manners, *Come Down from Yonder Mountain* (1962), occurs when two reluctant partners in a middle-aged romance catch a salmon but capsize their rowboat in Horseshoe Bay while trying to land the fish.

The title, *Come Down from Yonder Mountain*, is derived from a Tennyson poem but also refers to Grouse Mountain, on the slopes of which an assiduously self-sufficient widow from Calgary, Elspeth Wright, has rented a home to enable her eighteen-year-old son to attend UBC. Well-to-do and articulate, judgemental and imperious, Elspeth plans to continue dabbling in social work upon her arrival in Vancouver. These plans are soon complicated by two suitors in her unsentimental life, George Hodges, a charming but ineffectual social gadfly, and Eric Angus, a gruff and slightly roguish newspaper editor.

"In the soul of every woman, no matter how short her hair or how low her heels, lies a seed of romance, which if watered and nourished enough, will grow into a rambunctious, and often troublesome plant. Elspeth had no patience with romance. She liked her days crisp, flavoursome and well done, her nights cool, calm and quiet...Besides, two men in one's life were perfectly safe. It was only when the number dwindled to one that a woman's nerves were likely to suffer."

The urbane humour and Jane Austen-ish pronouncements on the foibles of the characters make this an extremely enjoyable book and certainly one of the most sophisticated novels ever set in Vancouver. However its dull jacket, affected title, apparently unadventuresome

content and old fashioned notions about women allow a reader with more modern prejudices to dismiss the writing as prudishly delicate and tame. *Come Down from Yonder Mountain* deserves to be critically reassessed and reprinted.

Margaret Walker, a native of Calgary, graduated from the University of Alberta and worked as a journalist and a teacher. She married, had three children and wrote *Come Down from Yonder Mountain* in Edmonton. Her whereabouts are unknown.

Another Vancouver novel of remarkably similar tone and from the same period, is Elsie Fry Laurence's *Bright Wings* (1964). The title is derived from a Gerard Manley Hopkins poem. When the daughter of a small town BC United Church minister announces she intends to marry an agnostic Jewish surgeon in Vancouver named Nathan Goldman, who is already married with two children, family conflicts naturally ensue. Though less urbane than *Come Down from Yonder Mountain*, this novel exudes the decidedly English charm of "sweet reasonableness," which makes it a worthwhile and truthful novel of manners.

Elsie Fry Laurence was born in England in 1893, ·educated in England, and tutored in Moscow for two years. Under the pseudonym of Christine Field, she published her first novel, *Half a Gipsy*, in London in 1916. She came to Canada and wrote mainly poetry, short stories and radio scripts. She lived in small towns in BC and Alberta before settling in Victoria.

NINETY-SIX

Ferry Terminal

6698 KEITH ROAD, WEST VANCOUVER

Jack Hodgins

At the outset of Jack Hodgins' first novel, *The Invention of the World* (1977), Becker, a BC Ferries employee, is at the mainland terminus "waving your car down the ramp onto the government ferry and singing to your headlights and to the salt air and to the long line of traffic behind you that he'd rather be a sparrow than a snail." In a Jack Hodgins' short story "The Crossing," set entirely on a BC Ferry entering Horseshoe Bay, one character finds Vancouver frightening, another sees it as a place for romance, and still another will use Vancouver as a place into which a Vancouver Islander can disappear. "Vancouver is our gateway to the entire globe," says Hodgins. "Conversely the ferry terminal is the point through which the rest of the world must pass in order to invade the Island. Consequently Becker in the novel beckons and invites the reader onto the Island, into the book.''

Jack Hodgins was born in the Comox Valley on October 3, 1938. He grew up in the little logging community of Merville. He lived in the Dunbar area while attending UBC from 1956 to 1961. ''Throughout childhood, growing up on Vancouver Island, I looked forward eagerly to living in ''the city'' where I expected to find myself amongst like-minded bookish people and stay forever.'' But Hodgins discovered that he was meant to live on the Island amongst the people he understood well enough to write about. He taught high school in Lantzville before turning full-time to writing. His first book, a collection of short stories, *Spit Delaney's Island*, earned the Eaton's BC Book Award in 1976 and national acclaim. His second novel, *The Resurrection of Joseph Bourne* (1979), a comic tale set in a coastal town called St. Annie (similar to Port Alice) won the Governor General's Award. A collection of short stories, *The Barclay Family Theatre* (1981) was also widely praised. Earle Birney at UBC was an important early influence; Bill New of UBC remains an important literary acquaintance. Hodgins' wife was born and raised in South Vancouver. He and his family now live in Victoria.

NINETY-SEVEN

Bowen Island

HOWE SOUND

Bowen Island, now easily accessible from Horseshoe Bay via a regularly scheduled ferry service, was home to Howard O'Hagan when he wrote one of the greatest distinctly western Canadian novels, *Tay John* (1939).

Tay John is a mythic tale of a halfbreed Messiah whose people hope to be led across the Rocky Mountains to be re-united with the peoples of the coast. The son of a mad trapper, he is born in his mother's grave without a shadow and ultimately disappears again into the earth with the body of a pregnant woman he had been living with. The story is narrated (a la Joseph Conrad, whom O'Hagan admired) by an English remittance man named Jack Denham, in the bars of Edmonton. *Tay John* borrows from Iroquois and Carrier Indian legends although it concerns the Shushwap Indians. The novel was originally published in England but fell into obscurity due to the onset of war. Re-issued in paperback in 1974, *Tay John* has risen in renown, particularly amongst writers, and now ranks as one of the most original classics of Canadian literature.

Howard O'Hagan

Howard O'Hagan was born in Lethbridge, Alberta in April of 1902. Although he formed lengthy friendships with Stephen Leacock and A.J.M. Smith while at McGill, and briefly practiced law, O'Hagan worked primarily as a guide in the Rockies and as a publicist for the Canadian National Railway and the Central Argentine Railway. A natural vagabond, O'Hagan met his wife, painter Margaret Peterson, in Berkeley. They lived together, unmarried, one summer on Bowen Island. O'Hagan then worked as a longshoreman in Oakland, California, at a gyppo logging mill near Cowichan, BC and on a survey crew in Kemano, BC. During this period he wrote wilderness adventure articles and profiles for American magazines like *True* and *Argosy*. A book of these articles based on historical figures, *Wilderness Men* (1958), contains an article about the legendary deformed and lecherous Cowichan murderer Tzouhalem. O'Hagan and his wife lived in Sicily from 1963 until 1974. They returned to live in Victoria where O'Hagan died in relative poverty in 1982. Talonbooks re-issued a collection of short stories, *The Woman Who Got on at Jasper Station & Other Stories*, and a novel, *The School-Marm Tree*, in 1977. Gary Geddes has also been instrumental in salvaging O'Hagan's literary reputation. O'Hagan told Geddes that he first considered writing as a vocation when he was a CPR guard for a trainload of 100 Chinese being taken to Vancouver in 1923 for deportation.

Almost half a century later, John Keeble's *Yellowfish* (1980) is a novel set minimally in Vancouver in which a protagonist named Wesley Erks is hired to convey illegal Chinese immigrants or "yellowfish" across the border from Canada to the US.

Bowen Island is also significant as the home of Einer Neilson, a frequent host to members of the Vancouver writing community in the 1940s and 1950s, such as Malcolm Lowry. Neilson saved Lowry's personal possessions, such as his phonograph records and his writing desk, prior to the bulldozing of Lowry's squatter's shack. Neilson telephoned prominent journalist Jack Webster and asked Webster if he'd like to have Lowry's desk. Webster retrieved it and possesses it to this day.

Einar Neilson (left) and Malcolm Lowry, Bowen Island

NINETY-EIGHT

1010

1010 CHAMBERLAIN STREET, NORTH VANCOUVER

Paul St. Pierre

Paul St. Pierre did most of his writing here in a log cabin office he had built on the three-lot property, which he referred to as Cardiac Climb in his newspaper columns.

Paul St. Pierre was born in Chicago, Illinois as a Canadian citizen on October 14, 1923. He grew up in Nova Scotia during the Depression. He arrived in Vancouver in 1945 to get a job as a wireless operator on a ship bound for the Japan war area, but the war ended. He has remained in BC ever since, well known as a *Vancouver Sun* columnist with a commission to rove all over the province. In 1952 he began to contribute award-winning scripts to the CBC television series, "Cariboo Country." His stories were drawn from his observations and experiences in the Chilcotin ranching area of the province, but "Chilcotin Country" was deemed an inappropriate title. He reworked his popular Chilcotin tales and characters into his first book of adult fiction, *Breaking Smith's Quarter Horse* (1966). The stoical rancher known only as Smith, the outlaw Gabriel Jimmyboy and Ol' Antoine comically evoke the manners and stubborn pioneering spirit of the BC interior in clever and often acerbic stories which pre-date W.P. Kinsella's somewhat similar use of rustic but smart Indians in his short stories. A typical "Smith" story by St. Pierre has rough-speaking ranchers gathering to reject a government offer of financial aid on the grounds that any help from bureaucrats will only turn into a hindrance in the long run. *Smith and Other Events* (1983) received wide critical praise and includes a short story, "Sales of a Small Ranch" that made St. Pierre the first Canadian writer ever to receive the Western Writers of America Spur Award.

Paul St. Pierre now lives and writes in Fort Langley. His other books are an adventure story for twelve- to fourteen-year-olds, *Boss of the Namko Drive*, *Chilcotin Holiday*, *Sister Balonika* and a coffee table book, *British Columbia—Our Land*.

"The official vision of Vancouver," says St. Pierre, "is that it is new and progressive, but here, in 1985, it is probably the last major city in Canada which does not have a traffic-free downtown mall. Black glass towers of appalling ugliness blight the downtown, perhaps one of the reasons that the downtown, after business hours, is about as lively as Toronto's downtown was, traditionally, on Sunday mornings.

"The strength of the city is in its spread of owner-occupied homes, almost every one of which has a fine garden, fresh paint, and a power boat, or camper truck, or both, standing in the paved driveway. The evidence of the good life is everywhere, almost as much in so-called working class areas as in the regions of wealth, but it is a privately-made and privately-held good life, not a communal one.''

In 1986 St. Pierre, a former Liberal MP for Coast-Chilcotin (a riding one-third the size of France), resumed writing a column in the *Vancouver Sun.* "I think you've got to have about ten books out, including three or four flops, before you're established.''

Burrard Indian Reserve Cemetery

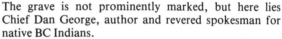

DOLLARTON HIGHWAY, NORTH VANCOUVER

The grave is not prominently marked, but here lies Chief Dan George, author and revered spokesman for native BC Indians.

Chief Dan George was born in 1899, a hereditary Coast Salish chief. He worked as a longshoreman for many years before turning to a career as an actor relatively late in life. He first appeared as Ol' Antoine in Paul St. Pierre's scripts for the CBC television series, "Cariboo Country." He performed in a Walt Disney film and gained widespread Canadian recognition for his performance in the stage presentation of George Ryga's *The Ecstasy of Rita Joe.* Then, for his role opposite Dustin Hoffman in *Little Big Man*, he was nominated for an Academy Award.

Chief Dan George was also ostensibly the author of one of the bestselling books from BC, *My Heart Soars* (1974), plus a follow-up volume, *My Spirit Soars* (1982). These were thin collections of poetic oratory instigated by local publisher David Hancock and illustrated by Mission, BC resident Helmut Hirnschall. In fact, according to his friend Hilda Mortimer, who published an earlier book on Chief Dan George, these books were ghost-written. "Dan George's writing was not really his own," she says. "He had a mentor and a guide who dictated most of what he uttered. This was a very erudite and warm Catholic priest who actually wrote most of what is in Dan George's books. It is ironic to remember Dan George as a writer because, of course, there was almost no tradition of that kind of literature for his generation at all." Chief Dan George apparently felt exploited by his publisher but told Mortimer he wasn't resentful. "I accept everything that life has to offer." He died September 23, 1981.

Chief Dan George

ONE HUNDRED

Malcolm Lowry Walk

CATES PARK, DOLLARTON HIGHWAY, NORTH VANCOUVER

Of Greater Vancouver's two literary landmarks honouring local writers (the other one being Pauline Johnson), by far the most important but least known is Malcolm Lowry Walk, a trail at the eastern end of Cates Park. As the misfit author of the most prestigious novel ever written in Vancouver, Malcolm Lowry lived and wrote in a squatter's shack that was located approximately 100 yards west of the boaters' dock presently at the base of Cates Park. David Nuttall, a Vancouver lawyer and author who lived in Deep Cove as a boy, accompanied his father, the local policeman, when he had to reluctantly serve Lowry and his second wife, Margerie Bonner, with an official notice to vacate. According to Nuttall, Lowry invited Nuttall Sr. inside for a drink. And Nuttall's father accepted.

Malcolm Lowry took occupancy of his beloved "little lonely hermitage" without plumbing or electricity in 1940 following his marriage to Margerie Bonner. In June of 1944 his shack burned down, destroying the manuscript of Lowry's second novel in the process. Lowry rebuilt the shack. "Although there was no questioning its hardship, at least in winter," he wrote, "how beautiful it could be then, with the snow-covered cabins, the isolation, the driftwood like burnished silver—the wonderful excruciating absurd shouting ecstasy of swimming in freezing weather."

Frequent visitors at Lowry's Dollarton shack were Vancouver writers Earle Birney and Dorothy Livesay. Lowry habitually despised the city of Vancouver, referring to it in his fictions as Enochvilleport, meaning "city of the son of Cain." On the other hand he referred to the tiny gathering of squatter's shacks on the foreshore of Burrard Inlet as Eridanus, a name drawn from the river in Virgil's *Aeneid* which waters the Elysian Fields of the Earthly Paradise.

The Lowrys left Vancouver for the last time in 1954, hoping to return. Malcolm Lowry's pier fell apart in the winter of 1956. The shack was quickly bulldozed in 1957 not long after Lowry's death in England.

Clarence Malcolm Lowry, Vancouver's most internationally venerated and critically studied writer, was born on July 28, 1909 in Birkenhead, Cheshire, England. Although he became an athlete and graduated from Cambridge University in 1933, he felt guilt for his inability to conform to his family's upper-middle class, Methodist background. At seventeen he left his hometown of Liverpool for a four-month trip to China as a cabin boy on a freighter. Wanderlust and alcoholism led to a permanent rejection of his father and England. Lowry initiated a student-mentor relationship with the American writer Conrad Aiken in Massachusetts; then he sailed to Oslo in 1930 to personally compliment Norwegian Nordahl Grieg on his novel, *The Ship Sails On.*

In 1933 Lowry published a derivative, seafaring novel, *Ultramarine,* which he came to regard as "an inexcusable mess." Initially inspired by readings of Eugene O'Neill's early plays, *Ultramarine* is a self-conscious search for identity. Its protagonist asks rhetorically, "Could you still believe in...the notion that my voyage is something Columbian and magnificent?" Lowry later conceived a lifelong cycle of novels to be called *The Voyage that Never Ends.* As an English Columbus exploring his own soul, Lowry would later naturally gravitate to British Columbia and Vancouver, a city often referred to at the turn of the century as the "Liverpool of the Pacific."

In 1933, after a trip to Spain, Lowry married Jan Gabriel in Paris, greatly impressed by the coincidence that she shared the same name with the heroine of his newly published first novel. This marriage was engineered by Conrad Aiken in the hopes that a wife would control Lowry's drinking. Before this marriage came asunder, Jan accompanied him on a ship that sailed into Acapulco harbour on the Day of the Dead, 1936, for what Lowry described as his "last tooloose Lowrytrek." Entering this New World of Mexico prompted Lowry to declare, "Like Columbus I have torn through one reality and discovered another." Lowry completed the first draft of his masterpiece, *Under the Volcano,* in 1937.

In 1938, due to immigration difficulties, Lowry went north to the United States. In Hollywood he met an aspiring mystery writer named Margerie Bonner. In 1939, due to his difficulty in attaining an American visa, Malcolm Lowry came alone to Vancouver where he was rejected for military service. He became desperately short of funds, dejected and ill. Bonner came to Vancouver to nurse him back to health. According to Bonner, the final and fourth draft of *Under the Volcano* was completed in their makeshift dwelling on Dollarton Beach on Christmas Eve, 1944. It was submitted for publication in mid-1945.

Under the Volcano is the story of Geoffrey Firmin, a former British Consul, descending into a New World Inferno on the Mexican holiday of the Day of the Dead, November 2nd (All Souls Day), 1939. The action occurs in the shadow of the volcano called Popocatepetl. The complex narrative traces the lives of the Consul, his estranged wife, his socialist half-brother and an

Malcolm Lowry

estranged boyhood friend. With an apocalyptic puritan-
ism Lowry intoned, "Yet no, it wasn't the volcano, the
world itself was bursting, bursting into black spouts of
villages catapulted into space, with himself falling
through it all, through the inconceivable pandemonium
of a million tanks, through the blazing of ten million
burning bodies."

Under the Volcano appeared in 1947. It was the first
of his many works to make direct reference to British
Columbia. Its protagonist is the owner of an island in
BC, a place described as a "genteel Siberia, that was
neither genteel nor a Siberia, but an undiscovered,
perhaps an undiscoverable Paradise."

Lowry's second most significant novel, *October
Ferry to Gabriola*, was edited by Margerie Bonner
Lowry from 3,000 pages of notes and published in
1970. It includes a poem of lament which symbolically
describes the English Bay Band Shell in Vancouver as
eternally empty, alone and locked. The concluding line,
"but still the old bandstand stands where no band
stands," is also the title of a chapter that bemoans the
scrupulous joylessness of a young city eager to harass
harmless drunks, annihilate old buildings and tame the
beauty of Canada's wilderness. Living above an
abortionist's clinic, the central character observes, "It
was a well-known fact the inhabitants of the West End
were so pure that they preferred to think they had no
natural functions at all."

Malcolm Lowry's other major Vancouver-related
fictions are a collection of short stories, *Hear Us O
Lord from Heaven Thy Dwelling Place* (1961), which
posthumously earned him a Governor General's
Award; *Lunar Caustic* (1963), published in the *Paris
Review*; and a sequel to *Under the Volcano* edited by
Douglas Day and Margerie Lowry, *Dark as the Grave
Wherein My Friend is Laid* (1968). His poem about
Hastings Street, "Christ Walks in This Infernal District
Too," is frequently anthologized. Lost Lagoon features
prominently in several stories. At the Vancouver
Aquarium, a wolf eel "with its expression of sadness
and the attenuated face of a prostitute by Edvard
Munch, uncurled its slow damnation, or hid its grief
beneath a stone."

Lowry wanted Vancouver to either return to nature
or grow up. "Are the people of British Columbia
unique in that they have never passed through the fears
and bewilderments of puberty?" he wrote. He particularly resented the antediluvian liquor laws which
required beer parlours to be divided into sections for
Men Only and Ladies & Escorts. "Nowhere in the
world perhaps were there similar places whose raison
d'etre is presumably social pleasure where this is much
harder to obtain, nowhere else places of such gigantic
size, horror and total viewlessness...within their

gloomy, music-bereft and often subterranean portals, you were obliged to drink nothing but that drink which of all alcoholic drinks perhaps most powerfully suggests gardens, song, merriment..."

Malcolm Lowry died, officially "by misadventure," in Sussex, England on June 27, 1957. His life and work have been the subject for innumerable books and academic studies. An interpretive documentary by Donald Britain is available from the National Film Board. In 1984, Vancouver screenwriter Michael Mercer's play about Lowry and Conrad Aiken, *Goodnight Disgrace* premiered to critical acclaim in Nanaimo. In the same year Vancouver poet Sharon Thesen published *Confabulations, Poems for Malcolm Lowry*. A film version of *Under the Volcano*, starring Albert Finney and Jacqueline Bissett, appeared in 1985.

But Malcolm Lowry is perhaps best remembered by his self-penned epitaph:

> *Malcolm Lowry*
> *Late of the Bowery*
> *His prose was flowery*
> *And often glowery*
> *He lived nightly, and drank daily,*
> *And died playing the ukulele.*

INDEX

Beth Hill

James Robertson.   Future work.

Andre Gorz.   Paths to paradise.